Published in 2013 by FeedARead
Publishing

Copyright © T M Patel

British Library C.I.P.

A CIP catalogue record for this title is available
from the British Library

"All events in this book are a mixture of fiction and non-fiction. All characters in this book are entirely imaginary and any resemblance to persons living or dead or actual events is purely coincidental"

Introduction

Imagine living under apartheid, imagine living in that world, but within that world there's another world. *The Immigrant: Stargazer* is a story that is based on the truth. The other world within apartheid is living in segregation with people of similar beliefs and ways.

Saesha is born in the outskirts of Johannesburg, South Africa. She is born into a Hindu family. She is a simple but bland child. She grows up slowly, living in a child's world and doesn't understand life and hardships in the real world and therefore the only thing she knows is her, her family and life in her town.

The Immigrant: Stargazer is asking to make life better for those living in **South Africa** and **India.**

The only people in this life,
that can love you and hate you at the same time,
or that you can love and hate at the same time,
is the family you were born in.
They are the people who are there first,
when you fail and win.
They accept you for your faults,
and forgive you for them.
They are the ones,
who have seen the road you've taken and battled.
Thank you for this family.

This book is dedicated to my family, and to a more
powerful thing out there which most of you refer to as
"God."
"I Love You"

31 December 1998, you're sitting on the outside pedestal wondering about life. Looking at your life is making you depressed. You think about everything that has happened up to now and today you are thinking a lot about Manav.

"I'm here on the outside pedestal,
the thoughts of your pleasant memories are becoming
so distilled.
Whether it's the end or beginning of years,
I admit you'll never fade.
Oh yes, you'll fade over time,
but through my eyes time is still,
and preserves our youth,
and determined love at that time.

You're moving on to third gear,
while mine's forced on fifth.
By the time I go,
maybe forever...
or come back we'd be so different.

Here I am sitting on this pedestal.
Usually when I think of you like this,
you somewhere nearby, or even passing me.
No more, now it seems to be.
Has your love died, or have you another?
Have our hearts lost track,
and no more twined?

Here I am sitting on this pedestal,
reminiscing of how it would be to feel you,
for I've never felt not one.
Now I strive to weigh a whole lot of love sliced to a

piece of lust,
still no matter how much,
the inevitable won't allow us to touch.

Once and forever burnt,
never stops, never fails,
from you I won't turn.
Even if I act as if you're nothing but some irremovable
stain.
This love I'll always have for you will be an
unforgettable flame. "

You, Nagma and someone else she knows are going to
spend New Years Eve together. Nagma has to be home
early tonight. It's the first New Year's Eve without any
big plans in a long time. You decide to have a night
picnic with some music in your front yard. Finding
friends and convincing them to come tonight was really
hard. "It's not as much fun as the outings I had on New
Year's Eve with Juhi, Chameli and Jayesh", mumbling
to yourself as you look into the sky. "Vivek is surely
having the time of his life, if only I could see Manav
tonight somehow." You had some pretty exciting
celebrations with Juhi, Chameli and her boyfriend. It's
nights like these when you miss them. It's nights like
these that you still wish to be with Manav.

The stars are out tonight, like most nights. It's a hot
summer's night. There are a lot of crickets making
noise as usual. You are lying on the blanket looking up,
"Why have you sent me to this world?" you ask looking
up in the sky. "Why fall in love if I can't have him?
Why become friends with people who can't see that
they've made a mistake? Why can't I find a job? I'm

nothing and nobody wants to be seen with me. Why am I here?"

You get up with the sound of footsteps. "Here we go again, no privacy in this place," mumbling to yourself. You get the car keys, Abhay knows you don't have any plans, he lets you use his car tonight after you tell him you've made last minute plans to hang out with some friends tonight.

Back in the Eighties

"Ke Pag Ghungroo,
Ke Pag Ghungroo Baandh Meera Naachi Thi
Ke Pag Ghungroo,
Ke Pag Ghungroo Baandh Meera Naachi Thi

Sa Sa Sa Ga Ga Re Re Sa Ni Ni Ni Sa Sa Sa
Ga Re Ga Pa Pa Ma Ma Dha Re Re Re Ga Ga Ga
Pa Ni Sa Pa Ni Sa Ma Pa Ni Ma Pa Ni
Re Re Re Re Re Re Re Re Ga Re Ga Re Ga Re Ga
Pa Pa Pa Pa Pa Ma Ga Re Dha Ni Sa Pa Sa Pa Ni Sa
Sa
Pa Ni Sa Sa Pa Ni Sa Sa
Pa Ma Pa Ma Sa Re Sa Ga Re Ma Ga Re
Pa Ma Ga Re Sa Ni Dha Pa Sa ... "

You remembered watching Bollywood films all your life. You remember how you and your sister laugh about this song, from the film Namak Halal, a 1982 Bollywood film. You are a tiny child and have short black hair, that ends before your neck. Your hair is really greasy. You have some kind of oil on it. You often hear your mum and your older sister refer to it as Amla Oil. You sleep with your mum before starting school. Your eyes are dark brown, they seem black. As a child, you don't care about style and looks. You have to wake up, get ready and go to school because that is what you have to do. You walk everyday with your sister to school. She wakes you up, and dresses you for school. It's hard getting up, and your sister gives you a nudge; well actually quite a few, and says to you, "Wake up." She knows you can't get up on your own, and she never shouts or screams at you.

9

Waking up to go to school is hard and you always want to sleep a bit more. She puts your socks or stockings on for you while you sleep, then your tiny little skirt, and leaves your tiny shirt for last. She pulls you by your hands, and that's when you know you must get up. She takes off your pyjama top and puts your shirt on, buttons it up and then puts your tiny tie on. She looks just like you. She means everything to you. You can't imagine life without her, she's always there for you. You both have a tiny body, the same haircut, eyes, and are very thin. She's taking care of you most of the time. You are a quiet and happy child in general. Your sister is more loud and open. Her name is Shalini. The Hindi and Sanskrit meaning of Shalini is "Modest." Sanskrit is a Holy and primary language of Hinduism.

You look up to Shalini and ask her things; in your eyes, she knows everything. She makes your lunch and sits you down for breakfast after you're dressed. Sometimes you both are late for school. Your school has a bell, and you and your sister have to be in school before the bell goes off. You remember seeing the last few kids near to the school walking coolly and then suddenly running for the gate when the bell goes off. When you start school, you love it. At first, you are afraid, but then see how fun it is to draw, paint, colour, and play. You don't remember your first day at school, and do not remember crying the way some kids do when their parents bring them to school. Somedays in class, you wonder what your mum is doing while you are here. You think of the toys that wait for you at home, especially one in particular; your cabbage patch doll. No matter how ugly she is, you can't separate yourself from her. You miss home and feel that school is now going to be your life. Your name is Saesha. In Sanskrit Saesha means "Meaningful life, and truth of life." Some say it also means, "With great desire and wish." Your mother comes from the state of Gujarat in India and she's Hindu. Your father too is Hindu. You were born in South Africa, in an Indian community, where there are many cultural and religious influences.

You don't know the meaning of happiness, why bore yourself with the word. You don't even know how to say or spell happiness. You cry, you smile, but know nothing about emotions or its roots. To you everyone around you lives in a world like yours. The world of a child with toys, paint, crayons and playing pretend.

"Abhay mera mota bhai"

"Abhay mera mota Bhai," is Hindi and means, "Abhay my big brother." Bhai is what you use in Gujarati for "brother." You call Abhay, "Bhai" and your other brother by his first name. Abhay is the oldest of all of your siblings. He is in high school. In fact you often see him at home in the evenings. His hair is pitch black, and very shiny. He has a lot of energy for a thin boy like him. His skin is a little darker than yours, from being in the sun, and spending a lot of time outdoors.

You often hang out with Abhay and his friends in an area in between a little passage and the garage. You often look for Abhay when you get bored. Abhay in Sanskrit means "fearless". Abhay's friends think you are pretty cute. Some of his friends bring you sweets and chocolates. At times Abhay's friends wait for him in the "sitting room", which is usually also referred to as "salon" in other homes. While they wait, you sit with them; they play with you or talk to you.

One day you wait with Abhay's friends while he goes to bathe. Since Abhay's friends bring you treats, you like Abhay's and their company. Your family has a cassette player in the sitting room. While you hang around with them they tell you to repeat some sentences after them; you watch them pressing something on the radio as you repeat the sentences. When Abhay returns they say, "Hey Abhay, listen to this!" They rewind the cassette and push play. They've recorded the sentences you've repeated after them. Your brother looks at you hurt and dissappointed. You realise you did something wrong. Your brother always treats you nicely and looks after you. Apparently, all the things said on the tape is what they asked you to say and repeat. It was all bad things, you didn't think they were going to do this to Abhay. You're too young, you don't even know the meaning of some of those words. You feel sorry for Abhay since he has very few music cassettes and the one his friends used to record you was one of his favourites.

Abhay gets a dog. It's from the house round the corner from yours, where you all go and play with your cousins now and again when Kalpana Masi comes. Kalpana Masi, Masi is the word that you use in Gujarati for aunty, referring to your mum's sister. At the house where you all play, there is a German Shepherd dog and it has given birth to puppies. The puppies are all thoroughbred. They give Abhay a puppy, and another puppy is given to Anuj Kaka. Anuj Kaka is from your mum's side of the family. Kaka in Gujarati means "Uncle". Sometimes when you meet distant family, and don't know what to call them you use the word "Kaka" to show respect. Abhay is so happy with his dog. He loves his dog. He calls him "Chunks." It is his dog and he makes it clear to all of you.

Chunks isn't allowed to sleep in the house at night. Abhay is worried since Chunks is still a baby. Chunks goes round the house with his puppy cry during the night since he's scared, and Abhay is scared that Chunks will wake the neighbours up. Abhay opens his room window and calls him. Chunks comes running. He consoles Chunks from his room window no matter how late it is at night. Sometimes when Chunks is very uneasy Abhay comes to yours and Shalini's room. He opens the window and stretches out his hand to pet Chunks. He does this for a while until Chunks is older and brave enough.

Chunks keeps you busy. Now you have someone to play with. Chunks hangs out more with Abhay and his friends. You talk to Chunks and sometimes give him Rotli when Abhay isn't around. In Gujarati, you call Rotli a type of bread, which is round and thin. Your mum makes Rotli almost everyday. In almost all Indian homes, rice, curry and other foods are accompanied with Rotli. Chunks is fun to be with and he is Abhay's best friend. Wherever Abhay is Chunks is there. He looks after Chunks properly, takes him on daily walks, and cleans up his poop. Chunks is a very happy dog.

The first year of school is fun; grade one, but later you have to learn how to write. You also have to go to Gujarati school after English school. When learning how to write, you are taught with the right hand, but you don't find it comfortable, and often change hands. When your father notices he is always saying something, which sounds like this, "Jamra haate lakvanu!" which means in Gujarati, "Write with your right hand!" When your grandmother comes, and finds you writing with your left hand, she tells you off. You change hands so often that you can write with both hands at one point and only change hands from left to right when you write in front of the elders at home, but always go back to the left hand when you are alone. In Gujarati school, you learn your mother tongue, and as you get older, you will eventually learn Hindi, India's national language.

In Gujarati school, writing with your left hand is also seen as something bad. You remember going with your sister to Gujarati school. At Gujarati school, you are afraid of one teacher. She looks so strict that when you walk in, look at her, you want to wet your pants. She shouts at the children so badly and at times hits them, or pulls their ears. It is worse than how English school teachers teach. You often sit with your dad. He revises things with you in Gujarati, and tests you. You know all the things in your Gujarati books on your fingertips, but still you are scared of the teachers. You hate mathematics. The teachers slap you instead of using canes in Gujarati school. The strict teacher that you are always scared of, points at a child in the class, and say in Gujarati, "You! What's three times fifty?," and that is when the fireworks start. She jumps from one kid to another, and you all have to answer in a second. Often you are lucky to get the easy ones. When she screams your name, you have to go running to her desk. Most of the time it's when you do something wrong, or have some answers wrong. When you get to her desk, you want to wet yourself so badly that before she can say anything, you say, "Prabha Ben can I go to the bathroom please?" This happened a few times. She lets you go to the bathroom when you need to, but when you come back you get the rest. Surprisingly, one day she stops shouting at you, she tells you your errors nicely. Ben means sister or teacher in Gujarati. Sometimes you refer to Shalini as ben. You all have to call the teacher by her first name followed by Ben. Some teachers are so strict and fat. You look at them and say, "I hope I don't get her, or her." You and your friends often laugh at the ones you don't like and say, "Jaari" which is a synonym for "Moti" in Gujarati, which means fat. Your friends at Gujarati school are different from the ones you have in English school. You recognise some faces in Gujarati school since you saw them in English school. At this time, you go to English school in the mornings, then come home from school, eat, relax or play a little, and then go to Gujarati school. Gujarati school ends at five o'clock in the evening. You just can't wait to come back from school so that you can play with Chunks. It seems like it's been years since seeing Chunks.

You do not remember when you started watching Hindi films but you already understood most of it when you were in grade one. With time, you realize English school is more important because not all kids come to Gujarati school. One day you and all the girls in your class have to get into one room and undress while the boys have to undress in another room. Some kind of health inspector comes to do a health check. This makes you very uncomfortable. You hope that there isn't anything embarrassing stuck to your panties, and stay still in one corner. You hate these kind of check ups. Sometimes health inspectors come to give vaccinations.

You are seven years old when, one day your father tells Abhay that he has to return the dog to the people who gave it to him. Abhay has to do it, and Abhay shouts, "Why don't they ask Anuj Kaka for their dog? Why must it be me who has to give Chunks back to them?" Abhay doesn't listen to your father, and exclaims, "I am not giving Chunks back to them!" Abhay is sad, tears are rolling down his face yet he tries to act tough, he's fighting to hold them back. You also don't like the idea of Chunks going. You know something isn't right here.

16

You just do not give Abhay a dog, which becomes his best friend and then take it away from him. Generally, in your culture you were all taught that when you give something to someone you do not take it or ask for it back. Chunks has to go back because a car hit the dog which belonged to the family who gave Chunks away to Abhay. Abhay goes to leave Chunks even though he is sad inside. You wonder, "Isn't there anything my father could do or say to stop them?" You all see Chunks leave that day. You all came to love Chunks, he was part of the family. Abhay tries for months to get Chunks back. You hear that Chunks isn't being looked after well by them. Abhay even tries stealing Chunks back one day. He manages it, and you all hide him away. You are so happy to touch Chunks again. You have a big smile on your face. You want to be with him everyday and touch him, hug him but that doesn't last long, somehow they find out and that same day they come straight to your house that evening to get Chunks back. Abhay loses hope.

At English school, you can't wait for break time. You are excited about what you have for lunch each day. You play on the school jungle gym during break times. It's newly built. Shalini comes to check up on you during break times and plays with you for a bit. She's also like a friend too, just in case you don't have anyone to play with. Shalini sometimes steals from other children your age. If you both are alone in the class, than she'd look in the bags of the other kids to see what they have and steal nice snacks from them. You are afraid of being caught. She makes you get the bags where you know kids have chocolates and other goodies. You are always scared and shake while bringing her the bag.

One day you take a boy's bag and you were about to hand it to Shalini when the boy who owns the bag walks in. Ever since, he keeps calling you a thief, and screams it out loud whenever he sees you on the road or at school. You are upset and tell Shalini, "The whole class will find out that I am a thief when in the end it's you." Ever since that day, you both stop stealing but the boy still keeps calling you a thief.

One weekend a young boy comes running to your house. He comes looking for your father. His face is serious and says, "Are you Abhay's dad?" Your father looks worried, and from the tone of the boy's voice you too get worried. You think your brother is in an accident. The boy says, "Abhay is hurt!" Your father's face changes, he is really worried. He looks as if his worst nightmare has come true. You think your brother is badly injured and you are very scared that you'll never see him again. When you see Abhay, you are so happy that you want to hug him, but pull back since it's a very strange thing to do. No one at home gives hugs or kisses to each other. Abhay hurt his kneecap while playing football with a group of friends in the field near your primary school. He has a thick bandage around his knee, after returning from the doctor's. You are a little angry because you think his friends did it purposely.

Sometimes you come home from school with bruises, some big ones, and at times small ones. You are afraid to show your mum, because you know she'll be very angry with you. If she sees it, she often gets angry and say in Gujarati something like "Kaam Vadayru". Which means "you've made more work." You don't understand her, and wonder, "How can I avoid getting hurt if another kid pushes me by mistake while playing." Somedays she's in a really bad mood and during those times you wonder if you or your siblings did something wrong. So watching how angry she is sometimes, you'll try to get out of the way or try to do things more perfect, yet at this age you don't know how much more perfect to be or what exactly you should be perfect at.

One day your uncle decides to take you to the airport. You are extremely excited, and go with him and his family. A few days after your mother tells you off. It isn't the first time. You really come to think that you're causing problems and can't understand what you did or said wrong. You start to make a habit of keeping quiet, but there are times you can't avoid it, especially when you get excited. When this happens often you get the feeling that you can't really say what you like around your mum's side of the family. Shalini and you like Kalpana Masi a lot; she is from your mother's side of the family. You hardly spend time with her, and these days you hardly ever see her. She has three kids. Her oldest daughter is a girl, and two boys. You remember going to play with them. They don't live near you but come to a house of the people who gave Chunks to Abhay, which is around the corner from your house. You and your siblings go there when they are around. They are just 5 minutes walk from your house. You see them on very few occasions. You get jealous when Shalini comes back from outings that she has with Kalpana Masi. Sometimes she comes back with a really nice haircut, and you ask your mum, "Why don't I get to go with Kalpana Masi?" You feel that you are probably not fun enough, but than realize, that you are not the right age to do somethings your sister gets to do, and that is why you don't get to go along with her at times.

You hardly see Abhay; he often comes home from school and drives your fathers Datsun. The Datsun is an old car that looks like a tiny box. It is orange in colour. It's old and has wires coming out from all sides. Apparently it is such an ugly car that when the robbers steal it, they take very little and leave it in a field close to where one of your cousins live. She calls your father and tells him that she thinks that the car abandoned in the field in front of their house belongs to him, and Datsun comes back home again. Abhay starts driving at fourteen years of age. He learns how to drive on his own. He loves everything about cars. Since the Datsun stays at home and your father is at work, Abhay drives around with it.

By the end of the year, there is a lot of tension at home. Abhay, fails the year, and does not want to repeat, in fact it's worse; he wants to leave school. You are really afraid, there's just so much tension at home. Your father is worried all the time. He isn't strict on Abhay but on this topic he's firm and tells him, "Abhay you have to study." and Abhay says, "Ok, I'll do a course in motor mechanics."

Normally everyone takes up a profession when finishing high school. The certificate one receives when finishing high school allows them to enter a University or College, depending on what they've studied or if they pass. Abhay says to your dad, "There is a motor mechanic course that I can do without finishing high school." Your father is happy, and this makes you happy too. You hate seeing this tension and frustration at home. You are also proud that your brother is going to continue studying.

During this school holidays Shalini takes you for a ride on one of your brothers' bicycles since you don't know how to ride one. You both often have matching clothes. You sit on the top tube while she rides. Your skirt catches in the area of the chain and crankset and you come home with a torn skirt but that doesn't put you off the bicycle, sometimes you both come home with torn skirts.

Why You?

You are eight years old, and in Standard one. It has been a while since anyone says anything about you writing with your left hand, this is a great relief. A second language is introduced in Standard one. Afrikaans, it is really difficult learning Afrikaans.

At school, you like a boy whose name is Vinesh. He lives near your house. You see him everyday because he is in your class. You like him a lot but he obviously doesn't know. You disguise it well.

One day Vinesh doesn't come to school, and the teacher asks loudly, "Who lives near Vinesh put your hand up? I need you to take some books to him." You wait for someone to put their hands up. You don't want to because you are shy. No one puts their hand up, so you take the courage and put your hand up. The teacher comes to your desk and gives you the books to give to him.

After school, you walked down the road to his big Mansion. You hope and think, "God I hope his mummy doesn't take the books from me to give it to him. I want to see him." When you get to his house, you press the doorbell. A young, beautiful, woman opens the door. You say, "Hello, I'm in Vinesh's class and the teacher gave me these books to give to him." She says, "Ok, he's upstairs, you can go up and give it to him." You realize that the young woman is Vinesh's mum. She is so beautiful. Her hair is long, black, and layered. It looks wavey and shiny. She looks so pretty in the Sari she is wearing. A Sari is a long material sometimes simple and sometimes very elegant. It is a traditional wear to Hindu women, which they drap around them. One often has a matching blouse with their Sari.

You head upstairs while his mum calls out from downstairs, "Vinesh, someone is here for you." You don't hear Vinesh's reply. If you heard his reply you would know where to go, after all it's your first time coming to his house. You reach the stairs and look for him. You come to a door, it's open... and you see something that you won't ever forget for the rest of your life...

You walk home from school with a far cousin; she is family from your mums' side. You sometimes hang around with her since she goes to her auntie's house on your street after school. You walk it together after school. Your far cousin comes from a rich family, yet it surprises you why she walks home and hangs out with you somedays. You never see her at the weekend just on school days.

One day your far cousin isn't with you, and a girl stops you. She is with her group of friends. You look at them quickly and put your head down, because you are afraid. They look rough. You really don't want to play around with them. You quickly scan through your mind to see if you have done anything or said anything that you should not have said to one of them. You can't think of anything and think they are going to bully you and wonder, "Why else would they come to me?" You really hate being tiny. You are afraid, and the girl says confidently, "Can you quickly go and buy me some chappies since I can't leave the school?" You say in your mind, "Wow that's it! Chappies, only Chappies" and breathe out a sigh of relief. You answer, "Sure, no problem." She puts the money in your hands. You scramble off moving your little ass as fast as you can before she changes her mind to bully you. You hear her scream, "The purple ones." You quickly get to the car that sells snacks to kids during break time. You realise that you didn't check to see how much she has given you. You hope that the money is enough. You hand the money to the man, and point at the purple gum, which everyone calls Chappies. You go back into the school gates and give the Chappies to her. She says, "Thank You."

As you walk home from school you think of the girl who sent you for the Chappies. You finally remember her name, Alaiarasi. She lives behind your street. She is friends with some girls you know at school who live in the same street as her, however they are not the same girls that hang around with her during break time. Alaiarasi in at least four Indian languages mean "Queen of waves."

A few days after your far cousin joins you again. Just as you walk out of the school gates, Alaiarasi comes running and asks you to buy Chappies for them. By now, you know it's the purple ones; you have been doing this job for the last few days now. You take the money and say, "Ok." Your far cousin asks you distastefully, "Who is that?" Proudly you say, "Well, just a girl who asks me to buy chewing gum for her now and again." This is your way of saying, "I have a bunch of cool friends." Before you can turn around and take the gum to Alaiarasi your far cousin says softly,

"Why don't you take one for yourself, and we can split it?" You say, "It doesn't belong to me." She says, "Oh! Come on! She won't know one is missing." You can't believe this is coming from your rich cousin. You have issues about saying no to people, and even worse to those insisting. You do it; you take one, slowly moving your hand over to your far cousin, your back is facing the school so you know they can't see you. You turn around, walk to Alaiarasi, and return the chappies like you always do. You are worried and thinking, "What if you get in trouble for it?" As you walk, your far cousin doesn't even wait until you're both out of sight. She takes out the Chappy and split the chewing gum with you and repeats, "She won't know it's missing."

The next day you are almost out of the school gate when Alaiarasi stops you. You wait for her to say, "Can you go and buy some Chappies for us?" Her friends are surrounding you and just then your far cousin says quickly, "I'll carry on." She's gone. You often don't wait too long for each other in case one of you comes out late from the last class. You know what is coming and so does she. Alaiarasi says, "I saw you yesterday, you stole Chappies from me." You hear chappies instead of chappy. You say, "No!" and are not given a chance to speak. They push you around and threaten you. This is now happening everyday. Your far cousin leaves you behind as you come out, she knows the routine. You wish you can go home but have to stick all this and usually get home late.

You think about what your far cousin said, and what happened that day. You curse her in your mind saying, "It's her that deserves to be here in my place, it should be her getting home late everyday." Now you really get a good look at Alaiarasi by seeing her everyday. She looks like a fish, with that fish plait. She has fat lips, and her skin is dark and rough. She is so ugly. Alaiarasi is too ugly to be called the "Queen of waves." As soon as you get out of class and try to leave with your far cousin, they stand right in your way, and you stop, since it's now a routine. They let your far cousin go; she quickly squiggles past through them. You look at her and think, "Coward!" You are terrified. You never have enough time to explain to your far cousin what's happening, because as you walk out they're already there waiting for you. You think now everyone is going to find out about this and you won't end up having any friends, even your far cousin will stop hanging out with you. You are worried that all this is going to happen to you, and that no one will even hear the truth. You go to your sister, and tell her what is going on. It is too much. You think deep inside she too is afraid of them. The weekend comes and Shalini and you walk on the street where Alaiarasi lives, and you say to Shalini, "I don't want to pass her house. What if she's there and starts bullying me worse than in school! At least at school I am saved by the bell." All grade ones, twos and Standard ones finish school early. You finish on the second lunch break. This is the last year that you will come out early. Next year you will be in Standard two and will have to stay in school for longer hours. Shalini says, "Don't worry, nothing is going to happen." Luckily, she is right, but as you pass the house on the corner of her street, you see the girls who she hangs around with after school. They stand with their mother outside and scream out loud, "She's the girl that stole Alaiarasi's chappies." They look at you dirtily. You just

26

put your head down as you walk.

During that year, Vivek wants to play teacher, and creates a school in a little space or passage next to the garage in the front yard. Vivek is your other older brother. Vivek in Sanskrit means the ability to discriminate between right and wrong, while in Hindi it means wisdom and knowledge. Vivek has short hair, dark brown eyes; they are almond shaped, just like the rest of your siblings, and like most people in the Indian culture. Vivek is fair, while you, your sister and your elder brother has brown skin. He doesn't look anything like you, your sister and brother. He doesn't look like your parents. He is not as skinny as you and your siblings. People jokingly say, "He's probably adopted." Abhay is thin compared to Vivek and boys his age; he looks like a boy from India. Vivek calls you "Darling." You hate that word, and fight with him because he calls you "Darling." "Darling" really does tick you off all the time. He loves the Hindu culture a lot. A new Temple was being built at the corner of the street and now that it's built, a new priest moves in with his family. His kids are in your school too. Vivek hangs out with the Priest's son a lot. He helps the priest and even wears the Dhotiyu. Dhotiyu is a type of traditional wear, which Hindu men wear sometimes, and often what Priests wear. A Dhotiyu is a long material over 4.5 metres long or even around 5 metres long. There are many ways that Hindu men can wear a Dhotiyu. Some of your friends see the school Vivek is starting, since the yard faces the road. It has a board and at least one table and some chairs. Vivek says, "Here you'll learn how to write cursive neatly." You don't know how you end up in Viveks' teaching programme but there you are. You think it is going to be fun playing student.

One day you come back from Gujarati school at around five o'clock in the evening. Your bossy friend happens to be with you, and joins Vivek's class. You have a bossy friend at Gujarati school, and a girl by the name of Mitali. Mitali in Sanskrit means "Friendship." If there ever exists a perfect friend for you than that's Mitali. Mitali always defends you in Gujarati school, and always saves you from bullies. You walk home with her after Gujarati school. You don't think that you are going to last long in Vivek's class. Normally Vivek steals your friends and then leaves you out of their plans. Strange enough, it is actually a very serious class.

Vivek teaches you to write cursive and shouts at you when you don't do it right. You write so neatly and beautifully at school, but that doesn't change that you are still average at school. Gujarati school students have a day where different kinds of doctors come down for free and do check ups on kids. Your dad takes you. A doctor checks you, and weighs you. You weigh fifteen kilograms. The doctor says to your father, "I need to take some blood samples." He takes some. You see your blood and it looks black, then the doctor sends you home. You go around telling your brothers and sisters, "I have black blood ...oooo I am an Alien." After that you were taken for another check up, everything seems fine now.

Now it's winter and around a certain time of the day the class smells. You begin to wonder if the smell is just around your side of the classroom, and don't know where it's coming from. You start to think the smell is coming from you. The moment you're sure about it you get nervous, this makes the odour stronger. As you get nervous, you concentrate less. You close your armpits more just in case the smell comes from there. Then one day, you close your legs tighter just in case the smell comes from there. Closing up the armpits or legs more in your mind means that the smell won't get out, but when you are tired and want to relax, it gets worse. Vinesh sits behind you and you worry that he will think that it's you who smells, this will just make things worse for yourself after all, you like him a lot. You worry about the fact that he won't ever look at you or be interested in you ever. You think of the eternity of school life you're facing. If your name spoils now, it's going to be spoilt for eternity.

As days go by, you realise that the smell comes from wearing stockings, thick green stockings, which is part of your uniform in winter. In winter, the mornings are cold but it eventually gets warmer in class since the sun enters through the window. You wonder if it's normal, this, what is happenning to you. You don't know if other children in the class have the same problem. You confide more in your sister then your mother. You are ashamed to talk about this matter to your sister, in case she embarasses you and tells your brothers or your mother, or perhaps she might laugh at you. You even convince yourself that perhaps your smell alone is not that big to make the whole class smell. Somehow you have an instinct that you're being teased, but don't know it for sure, so to be sure you decide to find proof. You sit in the front row and want to see how your classmates react.

One day just as the smell starts you decide to turn, you catch Vinesh making actions, he's putting his one hand on his nose. When you turn he stops when he sees you staring at him. You feel like an alien that day, you feel really bad. It is now a sure sign that you smell. Vinesh is never going to like you again. Sometimes you pray excessively before the smell even starts or if it starts earlier than normal, "Please god let there be no smell today, please let it go away."

In Winter your dad wakes up early to switch on the electric heater before you all get up to get ready for school. It's really hard waking up during winter. It's a habit to wake up, run to the sitting room, sit next to the heater and warm up your clothes. Shalini is usually the first one to dress, she then warms up your clothes, comes to get you so that you have warm clothes ready to put on.

Winter is gone and you don't ever want to see those stockings again. Now that you don't wear those stockings, the class doesn't smell anymore. You make a vow, "Next year I will be prepared for this issue!" Now that it's summer you don't smell anymore, but if there is a smell, another child is saved because it's easy to blame you. You wish and pray everyday on your way to school, "God please let there be no smell in class today. No smell at all." There's silence most of the way to school. You don't want to be there, but have to and pray that you'll have a good day. Vinesh still talks to you and you feel better. The nightmare is all over but it's still going to take a lot for it to be forgotten. "Next year I will give him a better impression of me and that way he might like me more," you hope.

Alairasi bullies you for so long, that you see another year of bullying coming your way. It seems like eternity, and you hate getting home late everyday. You get to a point where you hate your far cousin, and try telling Alaiarasi the truth for once, but she doesn't believe you. The truth doesn't matter anymore.

There are two sisters that you make friends with, you often hang out with them on an odd Saturday. They don't stay on your road but come to visit their grandparents and sometimes stay there during weekends. When they see you outside they call you over. They are like models. Both of them have long hair. It stops right before their butt. Their hair is like silk with some streaks of gold. They are tall and around Vivek's age. They have big almond shape eyes. They look like models and always have the latest fashion. They dress amazingly. Vivek also makes friends with them. Some of his friends are common friends with them too, so he too hangs around with them at times.

Your street has many children your age. Most of them are in the same school as you and your siblings, some of them hang out together at the weekends. At times they do things and invite you, and at times not. You hate it when Vivek comes while you hang around with them. Vivek often makes friends with your friends and leaves you out when they make plans to hang out and do something different.

One day you come from Gujarati school. Your mum gets you into the house in a hurry. Your dad usually comes home at six o'clock. You're busy wondering what's going on. You get in; she shuts the door, and locks it. You wonder, "This is strange, what about Abhay, Vivek and Dad?" This is not a daily routine. Your mum takes you and your sister and shoves you under the bed. Your mum also gets under the bed, and holds you and your sister tight. You wonder, "Dad should be here anytime now, why are we under the bed?" It all seems like a game until your dad comes and pushes the door handle. The door is normally open when he comes from work, you or someone in the house normally comes running to open it if it's locked, and usually it's you who comes running to the door when you hear the outside gate open. It's strange why your mum isn't going for the door, you try getting out, and your mum pulls you in. You look at your sister, and think, "Why isn't she trying to get out to open the door?" Your father screams, "Shalini! Saesha!" as he screams continuously in front of the house for you and Shalini his voice becomes desperate. "Shalini, Saesha, open the door." Now he comes around the house banging on every window screaming, "Shalini, Shaesha." This makes you cry. You think you'll never see your father again. You know he sounds worried and you can't understand why he has to suffer like this. You cry, and cry, and want to scream but you don't want to lose your mother either in case you scream. You don't know if this is right in the adult world, but as a child, this seems wrong. Something seems wrong. Your mum finally gets out from under the bed, and you think it's over and stop crying. Your brothers aren't around. You come running to your father, only to see the police at the door. Your mum was waiting for the police to come. That's when you realize something is really wrong. You never get round to finding out what the problem was.

32

You and Shalini take a walk sometimes. One day Abhay tells you both, "Chunks is in front of the house." You both say together, "What! The house where we used to play with our cousins?" Abhay says, "Well yeah! Where else?" You and Shalini run to the kitchen. Your mum is making Rotlis and you take a whole stack of Rotli's in your hand and say, "Mum it's for Chunks." You urge Shalini to rush so badly, after Abhay told you both where to find him, as if Chunks is going to run away. You both go running to the house. At last, you find Chunks there. He is tied to a tree. His tail is wagging non stop. He tries stretching when he sees you and Shanlini, but his chain is too short. He stretches as far as he can to get to you both, while you and Shalini stretch your hands through the gate to touch him. You manage to pet him a little but you, Shalini and Chunks get tired of stretching and holding that position. You want to pet Chunks more and are scared to go into the yard to touch him, in case the owners of the property chase you and Shalini away. You don't want to give them a reason to change their mind for leaving Chunks outside the house. That will make you sad and that will mean that you won't be able to see Chunks again.

Somedays you find Chunks tied around the tree all day, somedays he's not around. Sometimes he tips his water over and has none, and at times, he has plenty. He eats your mum's Rotlis like crazy. You wonder, "Do they even feed him?" One day you jump the fence and touch him. He sits there, all happy. Chunks has something to look forward to, for the day he'll see you. His whole expression changes when he sees you and Shalini.

Your father puts you, Shalini and Vivek in Afrikaans

tuition. Afrikaans is so important that if you fail the subjects, English or Afrikaans, or both together than you have to repeat the year. You are petrified with repeating the year. When you finish Gujarati school, you go for tuition somedays in the week. On your way to tuition, you pass the house to see Chunks. He's never around at that time. At first, you are scared of the lady who gives you all tuition, because it's your first time in tuition. You think it's like school, but tuition is actually fun. The tuition lady is a nice pretty woman. She is so patient. Once she teaches you Afrikaans her way, both you and her find that you are good at it.

Towards the end of Standard one, you and Mitali walk home one day after Gujarati school as you always do. She says, "Saesha, I'm moving." You exclaim, "Oh! Ok." At the end of Standard one, the teacher hints there are two places for third place this year. You aren't used to coming out first, second or anywhere in the first ten in class. You eventually get another hint; that this year you could be the one to hold the second third place. "It's impossible," you tell yourself, and pinch yourself to remind yourself that this is reality after reminding yourself of your tough times at school.

To your surprise at the end of the year school concert and awards, you get the second third place for the best handwriting in your Standard. You almost die when you get onto the stage when they call your name for the first time in your life in front of a hall full of people. You get onto the stage nervously, to pick up your award, and almost trip on a cable. Your parents are there, in the audience, you try to spot them quickly but can't. You don't ever remember them being this proud of you. You know it's not normal to come out third just for having the best handwriting, and wonder perhaps you didn't do so bad in the exams, at least not as bad as you think. Your award is a book, "Piggy goes to hospital." You read it over and over again. You still can't believe you came out third for once in your life. Your confidence goes up, as you look forward to the next year.

You believe that this award has given you a good and new impression where Vinesh is concerned. Just the impression you've been looking for. You know that in Standard Two you will have a new class, so you will be all mixed up again. "This is the time to start over again," you think.

During Standard one, your sister introduces you to her friends' sisters on some lunch breaks. You enjoy going with Shalini. She has so many friends, unlike you. You have fun with one of her friend's sister. Through her, you meet her gang of friends. They are different to the type of people you are used to being around. These girls are your age but not in the same class as you. You get used to hanging around with them. They treat you like normal.

At the end of that year, there is tension again. You are worried that Shalini is going to move onto high school next year. You have to change classes and have to make new friends. Your father is stressed because Shalini's report card says that she failed standard five. Shalini failed by a few points. The report card isn't good and she is nervous about repeating. You fail Gujarati that year. You don't want to repeat and face the embarrasment. You can't understand how you've failed Gujarati when you are so good at it. In fact you believed that you really did well in the exam. It doesn't make sense, however your parents aren't so worried about you repeating the year. Failing is like a competition in your house. Ever since you started school, you always remembered someone in your family failing. You wonder, "For once in our lives can we have nobody fail?" Watching the tension makes you not want to fail. Your father speaks to the school Principle, and he passes Shalini.

Shalini is going to high school. After that your own tensions disappear, they are small compared to Shalini's, you have never seen Shalini so worried. During school holidays Shalini helps your mother a lot in the kitchen. She even knows how to cook, almost all the Indian dishes.

Standard Two

You go praying to school in the morning, ever since last year saying, "God please let today be the day when Alaiarasi stops bullying me." It really seems like there is no god there. You now finish school the same time as Vivek. More hours in class, and you come from school dead. Abhay stopped going to Gujarati school for ages now. Normally many kids stop going to Gujarati school or drop out of Gujarati school, because English school gets more intense. Now school days are long and you still have many years until you finish Gujarati school. Nobody bullies you on the first day of school, you expect to see Alaiarasi. Shalini is now in High school.

So now, while walking to school, it's one prayer less in the mornings from all the other problems that you have at school. You stop hanging around with your far cousin. There is no Alairasi when you get out. You wonder what happened to her. You never see her again. You think, "What about her friends, surely, they can come after me," but there was even no sign of them. You eventually find out that Alaiarasi moved.

There are a whole lot of new faces in Gujarati school. You repeat because you can't move on with classmates who were with you before. You don't see Mitali anywhere. You remember your last conversation with her. You're mumbling to yourself since everything just makes sense now, "Damit Saesha! You thought she was moving to another house and perhaps she told you this just for conversation. She told you she was moving because she was going to move far away from you."

You get used to Mitali not being around. You ask yourself helplessly, "What can I do?" You don't know how to keep in touch with her and don't know where she moved to. You have a whole lot of new faces in English class too. Before you could barely handle mathematics, but now you seem so lost. Afrikaans is another difficult subject for you. Your father confides in your brothers a lot. He seems to have loads of plans for them. You and your sister are not in any of his plans. Things at home are changing.

You see Abhay more than before. Your siblings often pick on and laugh at you. One day Abhay asks you, "Who is our president?" You reply, "Mandela." They all laugh at you, while Abhay says, "You don't even know that." You feel like the stupidist child ever, and wonder, "Maybe at this age all my friends know who the president of this country is, and I don't!"

For many reasons you now try to avoid embarrasment and answers, even at school. You start hiding your problems from your siblings even more. Standard two is hard. Your brothers seem to know everything, and sometimes they even know how much money your father has in the bank. You wonder, "How come they know so much?" You are used to this and being a girl in this house makes you feel invaluable; you look around and observe how Indian women are treated. "This after all is the Hindu culture," you wonder.

Your permanent class teacher is a man who has a big belly, and grey hair. He can be strict and looks old. He doesn't seem nice at all. Your last year's class teacher was much nicer. She seemed much more patient than this one. You'd be surprised if your teacher turns out to be nice.

As the months go, things get tough. You get sick and go to the doctor. The doctor calls it diarrhea. You think diarrhea is some kind of major disease for you to stay absent from school, "What a strange word," You wonder. You now have a new problem. You do your homework daily but you aren't sure if it's right. Your new class teacher usually picks on you. You now go to school everyday praying to God saying, "Please God, let my homework be correct, please God!" Everymorning, but everymorning, the same old story. The teacher picks on you so much that you decide to use the immortal disease of "Diarrhea" to skip the days that you're sure almost all the homework for his class is wrong.

One day a girl in your class asks you, "Why didn't you come yesterday?" You say, "I had diarrhea." She tells you, "The teacher said in front of the whole class that he can't understand how someone as stupid as you got to third place last year." You can't believe that a teacher is capable of lowering you up to such an extent. A few days after your conversation everyone in class knows you had diarrhea, some people laugh right in your face. You decide to ask someone in the house what is diarrhea. Vivek tells you, "it's shitting liquid!" You tell yourself, "Damn, why didn't I find out what it was before telling people."

During break times, you hang around with the group of girls you met last year through Shalinis' friend's sister. On the first day of school you thought they didn't want to hang around with you, but when they saw you come to them during break time they were actually very happy to see you. A nice girl in the group buys everyone in her group what they wanted. She has loads of spending money. You stare at her smiling wondering how generous she is, she doesn't need to buy her friends, she has them, and that's why she buys them stuff. This friendship is a new one than the ones you were use to having.

In the group, everyone shares their lunch, and tries each other's lunch. You are a little embarrased about your combination. Shalini often puts mango pickle and cheese. You don't mind eating it, but think it's a strange combination and for that reason you don't want to share it. Sometimes in class with all the heat some lunches smell, so after your smelling experience you make sure it isn't yours. You stick with the group. When people see you with them, people in your own class start to think you're cool.

Some girls that you hang around with at break time, ask if you want to be part of the volleyball team. You aren't good at netball, a game similar to basketball, only Netball is a sport for girls. Netball is a common sport played in Commonwealth countries, and started in England in the 1890s'. During Physical Education, you all play netball however you suck at it and no one passes you the ball. It's for that very reason you want to try a different sport. Somehow volleyball seems more cooler.

You dress yourself now, those days of your sister dressing you in your sleep when you were six and seven

are now over. You make sure your uniform doesn't
have any stains. You have more uniforms because some
are from your sister. Thank God, the stockings from last
year are now small for you, you have new ones. You do
almost everything yourself. No greasy hair anymore
although you use Amla oil now and again, but never for
school. You are a little taller now, still very skinny.
Your skin is smooth like a baby, you and your siblings
have inherited your mums skin, smooth like the pretty
women in India. You don't smell this year, but you are
afraid of some people who were in your class last year,
that ended up with you this year might think it's you,
and blame you if something smells bad in class; this
would mean if they cause a rumour than everyone could
believe them and blame you. Vinesh isn't around this
year. You try looking for him. You don't want to ask
anyone where's Vinesh, because than you stand the
chance of being teased, so you wait for someone to say
it. You find that Vinesh is at different school.

Observing your sister everyday, you're wondering if
it's normal for her to do what women do at her age.
"Shouldn't she be studying?" you ask yourself. Your
eyes open up more and you start asking yourself
questions. You wonder why your mother doesn't push
her in her education. You worry that Shalini still helps
your mum but now more than before, yet school is
getting tough, especially if it is much tougher than last
year for you right now. You really wonder about her
future. Your mum is too busy making Shalini into a
woman. You can't understand it.

At times, you shout at your mum in front of Shalini.
You think perhaps Shalini is afraid of your mother. So

you stand up for her saying, "Mum, Shalini has to study, you can't keep making her do house work." Your mum ignores you. Shalini gets upset when you stand up for her. You both fight so much that you don't see the point in repeating your words. You feel like you're wasting your energy for someone who doesn't want to change and finally give up. You tell yourself, "Well it looks like she wants to do kitchen work, if that makes her happy than so be it!"

Your mum and your sister spend so much time together. You don't understand how come your mum doesn't have any friends. You also want to be with Shalini and your mum since you feel left out. They take walks alone and go to the park often. Sometimes you asked, "Can I come with you?" but your mum says no almost all the time. All this time it's as if your sister is bringing you up, and not your mother. Your brother steals your friends and your father really doesn't do much with you. When ever you ask if you can join your mum and sister to the park your mum says, "We are speaking about important things." It doesn't make sense. Your sister isn't hanging around with friends her age; she's hanging out with your mum. "Just what happened to my sister?" you wonder. There are days you are just bored out of your mind. You look for the two sisters and hang out a bit, but not a lot.

You didn't like Gujarati school so much. You don't like your name. No one has the same name as you. There are always two of the same names in the class, or you would always hear of another person with the same name, but Saesha, is a name that no two people have. You wish you were named something much easier to pronounce. People that are not familiar with your name say Saaa-ei-sha; when it's plain old Seh-sha. The "eh" in Saesha, is like an "eh" sound. You often wonder, "Come on how difficult is it to pronounce that?"

Your father is going to get a new car. He is going to sell the Datsun. It's old, so old that it needs warming up in the winter for a good few minutes before starting to drive it.When you hear your father is going to buy a new car, one straight out of a box, you flip. You are so excited with the idea. Abhay is the most excited. He says, "I'm going to drive that car!" In fact Abhay convinces your father which car to buy already. Abhay is sixteen and knows a lot about cars. He comes home early from motor mechanics school. In the afternoons he hangs around with his friends in front of the house. You think that you all are rich, because your father has money to buy a brand new car. Vivek and Abhay seem to know a lot about your father's business than you and your sister do. You wonder, "How unfair this is, to be a girl, do girls even have any value in this culture?" It is now decided, your father is going to buy the car Abhay tells him to buy; Toyota Corolla, 16V Sport.

When the car arrives, it's amazing how beautiful it is. Your father also buys the insurance for it. Abhay looks after the car as if it's his. Abhay drives it more than your father does. Your father is used to Abhay driving it. Abhay has been driving since fourteen years of age . "At least papa has a reliable car now, we can also go for more outings," you wonder.

You go on picnics with your family. You especially like hanging around with Dharti kaka's family. Dharti, in

Hindi means "earth". Dharti kaka loves the outdoors. Your cousins there are around your age, they are two sisters and one brother. Most picnics are done with your dad's side of the family, or only your family. You never do picnis with your mother's side of the family.

You have memories of you being young, sitting on your mum's lap in the front seat of the Datsun. You used to ask your father happily, "Where are we going for a picnic?" It often was the same place as always in Roodepoort. As your father drove along you would look at the roadsigns and also learn how to read them. Sometimes you would scream and tell your father loud when you saw the first sign for Roodepoort from far, and at times, you would just fall off to sleep as you looked through the window. After watching "Jaws", you never learn't how to swim because you had fear of sharks. If Dharti kaka forced you to get in the water, you cried. Your dad always came to save you. He tried to teach you things, but you were so scared so you just wanted to be left alone, and mostly dry. Dharti Kaka sometimes took you all in his caravan to places. You remember being six years old when you all went to Durban. You had fun with your cousins. You even used to stay over with your siblings at their place during school holidays.

Abhay stopped staying over a long time ago. Shalini and Vivek still come and stay over with you. Last year Dharti kaka found out that you didn't know how to read time, so he taught you. Ever since then you could read the time. You used to like staying there but recently your cousin became bossy, and at times, she hit you. She threw big tantrams. Now Shalini doesn't want to stay over. At least Vivek still stayed over, but he isn't as nice to you as Shalini always is. To Vivek it's like you are in his way all the time. You can't understand why Vivek is like that.

It now comes to a point where even Vivek stops going to stay at Dharti kaka's house. This means that you won't get to stay over, even if you wanted. You can't understand why no one came to stay at your house. Sometimes you'd think, "Is my house that ugly and disgusting that no one wants to come?" You remember Fai's daughter came once, and never again. Fai with the pronounciation "Fauey" is what you all call dad's sister. Nobody wants to stay at your house it seems, and for that reason you and your siblings always want to go to Dharti kaka's house. You all had more fun there. You once made flower necklaces with your cousins and sold them for fifty cents each. Surprisingly enough so many people bought them from you.

Toyota Corolla, 16 Valve Sport

When the new car comes, it's normal to perform a "Pooja." "Pooja" is a ritual that Hindus do, that involves praying too. Normally a Priest can do the ritual, but some people do it on their own, at home. The Priest does a "Pooja" when you buy a new home, car, new appliances, temple ceremonies, festivals and weddings. It's done to protect the car and other appliances against bad influences. Often coconut water is used in a Pooja. Your mum performs the ritual and blesses the car. You love the car so much, that when you see it you look at it as if it's the fastest and the most beautiful car in the world. As soon as Abhay comes from the motor mechanics school, he takes the car. He drives around with it most days, and usually brings it back before your father is back from work. Somedays he can't take the car because there isn't enough petrol.

One day you come from school, after a while you see your father walk in. You ask, "Dad, why are you home so early?" He doesn't answer you. He is in a rush. There is a lot of movement around the house, and you find out that Abhay is in an accident. Luckily, nobody is hurt, but the biggest worry is that he doesn't have a driving licence. The accident took place on your street, further down the road, and you can't see that far from your front gate. You remember seeing an uncle that you saw now and again. He came to help your father. This uncle is a close relative to you all, he is on your mothers' side of the family. You are all told to stay at home and not to come to the scene of the accident. Your father finally comes home in the evening. You didn't go to Gujarati school that day. You still don't see your brother that day. The car is towed to the house. It's completely finished. As soon as things settle down, your father doesn't say a word. That's quite normal. Most of the time he doesn't tell you all what you all need to know. He only tells the boys everything. Your mum doesn't know anything and it seems like important things like this isn't discussed at home.

That evening Abhay comes home very late, and as the days go by you find out what's happening. The car is a complete write-off, and your father had to pretend to be the driver, because that's the only way the insurance can settle the claim. Abhay smashed into the Principle of a school some of your cousins go to. He wants money and in return, he will keep his mouth shut about who the real driver really was. Your cousins don't like the principle of their school and tells you, "Almost everyone complains about him!"

You go outside and look at the sad Toyota Corolla, which you often visit and touch. Now its eyes are smashed in. The insurance company will take the car away over the next few days, and is going to repair the car. Abhay tells your father, "The car won't be the same again, even after they repair it. It will start giving problems, you'll see." You have no car for one month and a half until the Toyota Corolla shows up again. When the car is returned, your mum hides the keys but Abhay finds them. Your father trys to hide the keys before he goes to work. Abhay wants to drive again but always finds the keys. Your mum has no way of stopping him; he won't listen to her. She isn't strict enough on him. There is a lot of tension between your father and brother; it's all in silence in front of you, as

47

you never know what is really going on.

Now you are in the Volleyball team. You all have to wear your Physical Education gear. White shorts and white T-shirt. The popular girls wear really short shorts, and you are so embarrassed of your skinny body, even the smallest shorts look big on you. You use your sister's shorts since they are longer. Your mum tries buying you and your sister some tablets to help you both gain weight, but at the end she tells you and Shalini, "I was skinny like you were when I was your age." You are scared to be the tiniest person on the team, and luckily, you aren't. Somedays after school you practise Volleyball. Some boys tease you, but you just ignore them and they'd stop, one in particular won't give up teasing you.

Since everyone thinks he's cool, and for him most girls in the Volleyball team are pretty cool, you too want to show that you are just as sleek as other girls in your team. His name is Clive. Clive is Christian. His sister was once in the same class as Shalini. Clive has very short hair, a little dark in complexion, loud spoken, sporty and for some reason he is cool. One girl in the Volleyball team likes him alot, she's pretty popular and argues a lot with another girl in your team. You wonder, "Just how can they play for the same team if they argue so much?" Finally they settle their differences. You can't believe it. You are part of the school's team. You play against different schools. When you think of the name Clive, some quick rhymes come up. You use to hear some of his conversations and your mind remembers some key words that rhyme with his name. You don't dislike Clive or anything but

48

the same old rhyme just keeps coming up. You say, "I must finish the rhyme, surely he'll find it funny." It goes as follows:

Christian Clive,
ate some rice,
he was nice,
he was cool; and precise...
and this would be a real surprise.

One day in Volleyball practise, Clive starts to tease you again. After the game he still continues. You say jokingly, "Clive listen to this, just listen. Christian Clive, ate some rice, he..." "Wait a moment, you're making fun of my religion." Clive says angrily. He repeats angrily, "You're making fun out of my religion huh?" You say, "No, I ..." He doesn't let you speak. You tell yourself, "Great Saesha, now that went really well!" You don't dare to continue with the rest of the rhyme after that. You honestly thought he'll find it cool. "It could have been worse, what if he thought I was teasing his name. Don't ever say your rhymes out loud again," you tell yourself. You make up rhymes for so many people, not because you're making fun of them, but because they come to you easily. After this event you are convinced that your rhymes are stupid. You stop yourself from making them.

In Volleyball, you are surprised at how tiny you are yet capable of playing this sport. The ball stops hurting your hands once you get the trick. You have one problem though; when it's your turn to start, you never can get the ball across the net. You always see the dissappointed look on your teams face. Every time you start the game. The ball always comes down right before the net.

It's your first match. You are worried about the start. You have practised so much and this means a lot to you. "Seasha you can't dissappoint your team," you wonder. It's your turn to start, your team mates are cheering you on, "Come on, you can do it." Deep inside you feel that expectation they have of the ball getting across the net but know you've never done it.

You look at the sky for a second; take a deep breath in, and wish it from your soul. You close your eyes and hit the ball, you open your eyes and for the first time in your life, the ball is actually flying across the net. You are applausing for yourself, the team is surprised while the girl on the other side hit it. The game goes on, but you are still shocked about getting the ball over the net. You never smash the ball. You still aren't at that level; you'll position the ball for a smash. That day your team win the game. You like volleyball more than netball since there you feel like a team and a member who actually contributes.

One day your Standard two class teacher comes to your house. When you come home from Gujarati school your sister says, "Your teacher was here." She says the teacher's name. You are so afraid. You say, "Why?" You thought he came home to speak to your mother. Your sister says, "He wanted a book, so he came with me to your bag, and as we took the book out, a big, green, grasshopper came out with your book. Your teacher got a shock. I almost slapped it with your book, but realized it was dead. By the way, why did you have a grasshopper in your bag?" You answer, "I have no idea how it got in." You pass standard two. You seem to scrape all the other subjects, but fail mathematics. You don't know how you've done it. You don't know how others study, you see Vivek study but only with his schoolbook. You don't know how to study. No one taught you how to study.

By the end of Standard Two, the Toyota Corolla 16V Sport gives constant problems with its alarm after the insurance fixed it. Abhay tells your father that it's better to sell the car before more problems arise. You can't believe that Abhay still has a say and more surprising your father still listens to Abhay as if he is someone older and mature.

Abhay finds a buyer, and the buyer wants to pay the first half in the beginning and the second half afterwards. The deal is made in cash and the car is now in their possession. You have doubts and don't think a deal made in cash is a good idea. You wonder, "What if the man has a problem with the second half of the payment? My family won't be able to do anything because the car will be in their possession." You try telling your father but he looks at you as if you are stupid. It frustrates you that he doesn't tell you more, because if he did perhaps you can help Abhay and him more.

More and more it's becoming clear that a woman's or in your case a girl's opinion is not welcomed, your father only listens to your brothers, and for the three of them it now seems that women in your home don't know about business, shouldn't know about business and couldn't make decisions on business, especially when it comes to cars. It is a topic, which a man must handle. The buyer is a young man; and he finally comes to pay the final amount to Abhay. Abhay had to run behind him for the money. When he paid the final payment he leaves swearing. You come out of the house to see what's going on. The man swears at Abhay, and drives off. Abhay swears at him back in his defense.

Nancy

You are in Standard three now and still going for
tuition. Now you have to take tuition for Mathematics
and Afrikaans. Shalini is with you in Mathematics
tuition but not in Afrikaans anymore. You hate
Mathematics and the tuition teacher is strict. No matter
how many times she shows you how to do certain
equations you never get the point. Your Afrikaans
tuition is more fun, the woman is so nice and the same
teacher as always. She has three sons, they are around
you and your sibling's age. They even have a cat, which
you want to play with the whole time. You like it so
much, and often run to pet it when your tuition teacher
goes away for a bit. The cat often sits on the sofa
looking outside the window. Towards the end of the
year, you don't go for tuition anymore.

Your Afrikaans tuition teacher's cat has kittens. She
asks you if you want one. You are so excited and want
one so badly. You already have a name for it. You ask
your father if you can have one. You beg him and say,
"Please Papa, please can I have a kitten? I promise to
look after it, bath it, and clean its mess, please!" He
says, "Ok." You take the kitten and name it Nancy.
Abhay doesn't like cats; he has ideas about having a
dog. Your father doesn't want the cat in the house at
night and manages to find a little house for the cat
outside. You think Nancy is still too small to be left
outside alone.

During the day, Nancy is with you but at night, she
meows loud and non-stop. The first day is the worst.
Her crying attracts other cats and within minutes, your

house is surrounded with meowing cats. You are afraid that the wild cats are going to get into Nancy's house, kill her, and eat her. You hope Nancy doesn't think that you've abadoned her. You can't sleep at night.

Every night Nancy cries and the next morning you feel guilty. You rush yourself, especially before going to school and after you're dressed, you rush outside to set Nancy free before going to school. You have a sense of relief to see her alive every morning. You remember your brother used to bath Chunks, and so you try to bath Nancy one day.

You fill the area where your mum washes clothes. Your mum washes clothes by hand. When you were little you remembered bathing in there too. You take some warm water in your hands and try pouring it on Nancy. She doesn't seem to like water. You manage to wet her a bit. You pick her up gently and hold her close to the water. The water is warm. When Nancy sees the water, she goes crazy and look like she's being electrocuted. You hold her by her tummy and she paddles her back legs so fast in circles, the way a person does when riding a bike. Her hair is dead straight and look pointed at the ends. You try bathing her, and she meows hysterically. It is really hard to control her. You try putting her down on the dry part of the sink, but she's clinging onto your clothes. You manage to free her claws from your clothes and place her on the dry part of the stone sink. Her claws grate against the stone sink as you tried bathing her. She meows hysterically and tries to escape.

Your mum sees the drama from the kitchen window

and screams in Gujarati, "Bilari ne khem chiara karé?" which means, "Why do you keep making the cat scream?" Nancy scratches you, jumps off the sink, and runs off screaming in seconds.

Two months goes by and you find out that Nancy is female. "Gosh I didn't see if Nancy was a girl, just imagine if she turned out being a boy," you wonder. Nancy starts to close the area where she leaves her faeces with sand. Abhay hates cats and often makes fun of Nancy.

One day as you come home from Gujarati school, you walk behind an African man who has a big sack on his back. A kitten falls out of the sack. You pick it up and hand it to him. He puts his sack down, and opens it to put the kitten in, you stand there watching and to your amazement you see a whole lot of kittens inside the sack. Your eyes open wide. The man asks, "Do you want one?" You say, "Yes." You have your eyes fixed on the white one, you point and say, "That one! Can I take that one?" He takes the kitten out and gives it to you. You take the kitten gently. You think it's a great idea, at least Nancy will have company, perhaps she'll stop screaming at night.

When Abhay sees Whitey, the new cat you bring home he says rolling his eyes, "Just great, two cats, a male and female, soon there will be kittens everywhere!" Abhay has a friend who he hangs around with often. When the two kittens are hard to control, your mum demands Abhay to help you. You drive them crazy while they run around in circles trying to catch your kittens. Nancy and Whitey, don't seem to get along.

During the day each one does their own thing. Whitey is a wild cat while Nancy is a house cat. You can't sleep at night; both cats meow and sometimes fight at night. You even try to put a board halfway trying to separate each other by dividing the space but it doesn't work. You worry and often ask Shalini at night, "Can't we do something else?" Shalini often helps you with things, but she can't think of anything else to do to stop them from fighting. Once the door is locked at night, there's nothing both of you can do. Your dad doesn't allow the kittens in at night.

One night, it's raining hard. The meowing is louder than ever. The moewing that night is louder than the thunderstorm and it sounds like the two kittens are fighting longer than the other nights. You and Shalini hardly sleep the whole night and you can't wait for morning. As soon as you get dressed, you run out to let Nancy and Whitey free. Shalini comes running behind you. You usually just open the roof and the kittens jump out. When you open the roof this morning, you see Nancy still on the floor, and in front of her is a hairball. Whitey jumps out. You pick up Nancy with your little hands and she's not breathing. You cry, "Nancy wake up, come on wake up!" but she's still. She's dead. You are angry at yourself and tell Shalini, "I could have stopped this, if only I was brave enough to open the door and go out in the dark myself, Nancy would still be alive now." You cry, time is running out and you have to go to school. Whitey is looking at you excitedly. He waits for you to pet him. You put Nancy down and look at Whitey angrily. "You did this!" you scream looking and pointing at Whitey. Whitey still looks at you excitedly and innocently. You and Shalini are both upset with Whitey, after the sounds you both heard last night; you are both convinced that Whitey killed Nancy.

Shalini gets a baseball bat and hits Whitey; she hits Whitey so hard that when he gets up, he heads straight to the drain in front of your house. You don't want to see Whitey ever again. You loved Nancy so much. You saw her growing up, starting to climb trees, sharpening her claws. You blame yourself for everything, and are angry with yourself for not protecting her more. Nancy was like your baby. "She is innocent, why did she have to die? Why did I bring Whitey here? All this is my fault"

You can't bury Nancy since you don't have enough time. You and Shalini have to go to school, or else you'll be late. "Come on Saesha, we have to go we'll bury Nancy when we come back," says Shalini. You don't want to go, you want to bury Nancy. Your mum comes and sees what the fuss is all about. "Mummy, can I bury Nancy and not go to school today?" "I'll tell Abhay to bury Nancy for you," your mum replies. You and Shalini make your way to school. You really don't want to be at school, you are so unhappy and remember all your good times with Nancy.

You can't concentrate the whole day at school. You get back to your senses and feel sorry for Whitey. Now Whitey is never going to come back, or trust you and Shalini again after being hit by a bat. You can't wait to come out of school. You want Whitey back and feel sorry for him since he's still a baby. When the bell rings you try to get home as fast as possible. When you arrive home you don't see Nancy's body and presume she's buried. You don't have enough time, you hurry up and start looking for Whitey. There is no sign of him. You don't know where Shalini is and need help to find Whitey. You go to the drain, and call his name. You have to return home, and get ready for Gujarati school. You don't want to go to Gujarati school but have to go.

When you come back from Gujarati school you hope to find Whitey. You ask Shalini if she saw Whitey. She says, "Yes he came back for some food, but I chased him away." You feel sad, and hopeless, "That's it, I will never see Whitey again." Abhay buried Nancy. You ask your mum to make you an oil lamp every night. Your mum or Shalini lights up the lamp for you since you don't play with matches. You put the oil lamp on Nancy's grave and leave it to burn every night and talk to her for a while. You tell her how much you miss her.

Your mum knows that she has to make you an oil lamp every night since you make a promise to yourself that you'll put an oil lamp on Nancy's grave, no matter what. One day it rains heavily, you go out, protecting the lamp, and put it on Nancy's grave. It goes off, you scream for Shalini to help you to keep it on. You both try everything to keep it alight but you can't.

It's not even a month, you find out, that Nancy isn't buried there; Shalini tells you that Abhay threw her in the outside dustbin the same day she died. You are furious, while Shalini and Abhay laugh about it. They find it funny that you put oil lamps every evening on an empty grave.

Eventually you slowly get over Nancy's death but blame yourself for her death and also for abandoning Whitey. You often think about it, and there's a feeling inside you that keeps making you feel bad, that you can't understand what it is. The feeling is so painful, and causes you to think over and over again, about how you didn't do enough to protect Nancy and prevent all of this.

One day you take a walk with your sister to topshops. You often call downtown, topshops. Shalini knows where the petshop is, and she takes you there. You see chicks, rabbits, birds, fish, dogs, cats, and hamsters. You see a puppy. You like it a lot and ask the man at the counter, "How much is the puppy?" He gives you a price.

Another day you ask Shalini to ask your dad for money. Since it's too much money, you plan to ask your father for the other half yourself. Your father gives you and Shalini money. Shalini knows what the money is for. You want to buy the dog. You wonder how Abhay will feel when he sees the dog, after all he loves dogs and the dog looks like Chunks. "Perhaps Abhay will even help me look after it," you wonder. Shalini liked the dog too so she takes you to the pet shop. You go in and look for the dog. When you find him, you say to the man at the counter, "I want to buy that dog," looking in the direction of the puppy. The man comes to see which dog you want. You point at the dog you want. He takes him out and puts him into your hands. You and Shalini pay for the dog, and off you go. Everyone likes the dog, even Vivek. Abhay asks you, "Is he vaccinated?" You say, "I don't know." The dog is fine, but in the second month, he falls sick. He's having stomach problems. You beg Abhay to take him to the Veterinarian but he doesn't want to. You are so worried and keep begging so much that finally Abhay takes him to the Veterinarian. "The Veternarian said that he must drink coke with a little bit of Alcohol," says Abhay. Abhay gives him some, and your dog isn't walking straight. Abhay and his friends are laughing at the dog. You hope your dog is going to get better.

The next day you come back from Gujarati school. You don't see your dog anywhere. You ask Abhay, "Where is the dog?" He says, "It died." You don't believe it. You wonder, "How could it die so quickly? The Vet checked him." Abhay doesn't tell you how he died. Nothing makes sense.

Some months go by, and it's school holidays. One day you ask your father for money again and than you ask Shalini if she can take you to the pet shop. She says, "Ok" and you both go walking to the pet shop. You buy a white rabbit and call it Nancy. Again, the rabbit isn't allowed to stay in the house so you have to leave it outside at night. You put the rabbit in the house where Nancy and the dog once lived. It gets so windy that you are worried perhaps you didn't secure the roof properly. You hear a sound and you're uneasy that perhaps the roof of the house flew off, shortly after you hear some wild cats outside. If that's so, there's no saving Nancy. The wild cats will find her since they've been around during the other nights because of her scent, You don't want to go out at night, you are scared, and also if you do, you might alarm the whole house if someone wakes up hearing you open the door. You can't do anything and try to peek from the window to see if the roof flew off, but it's so dark that you can't see. You hope not since you put loads of rocks on the roof. You just can't sleep yet sleep takes over.

You wake up late the next morning, and go outside. You find your mum hanging the clothes on the washing line. Your mum says, "Nancy isn't in her house. The roof flew off last night." You are worried sick. "Perhaps the cats found her. There is no blood, no sign of Nancy. Come on think Saesha, think where can she be?" You quickly run to the spot where she often hides, behind some bean plants, often difficult for any cats to get through. There she is, you pick her up and feel her heart beating quickly. Your mum allows Nancy to stay in yours and Shalini's room, as long as she's in a box.

That night you are really happy to have Nancy in your room. You sleep well, and have no worries. You get up the next morning, and just as you are about to put your feet on the floor, you see little black round balls all over your room. You scream, "Shalini, Shalini." Shalini says sleepily, "Hmmm what!" You exclaim, "Look at the floor!" She peeks from one eye and quickly gets up in shock. You both look at each other. Nancy shat everywhere. Now you know why the room door is shut. Someone had shut the door to make sure Nancy stays in the room with you both. Coming out of the room is like coming out of an area full of booby traps. Your mum shouts at you and orders you to clean the mess. Shalini helps you to clean the mess.

Somedays go by and you think that Nancy is boring. You can't do much with her. She eats and shits all the time. You could play with other animals but can't do much with Nancy, yet Nancy is the easiest to look after and actually lives longer than others.

One day Shalini has to go to topshops again. You ask if you can come with. She says yes. You both walk into the petshop, and look at the animals. You see some rabbits, birds, but most of all a kitten catches your eye. You ask the man at the counter, "How much does the kitten cost?" He says, "Fourty Rands." You think, "That's cheap!" The next week you ask Shalini if she can come with you to the pet shop again.

You ask your father for twenty rand. You decide to take Nancy with you to the pet shop. You tell Shalini you want the cat. You both walk into the pet shop again. You look for the kitten to see if it's still there. When you see it's still there you ask the man at the counter, "Sorry Mr, I bought this rabbit from you over two months ago, is it possible to change it for that kitten?" The man looks at you and Shalini in silence. You say, "I have twenty rands more." He says, "Ok," Nancy costs a little over twenty when you bought her. You ask the man at the counter, "Should I put the rabbit with the other rabbits?" He says, "Yes." As you put Nancy down with the other rabbits, she stands up on her two legs, stretching out her front paws towards you. You are sad for a second yet happy to have a kitten again. As the man put the kitten in your hands you say, "Thank you" and leave. You don't need to buy food, because you still have some cat food left. "The kitten will be less to worry about, at least it could stay outside and it's a little bigger than Nancy," you think.

After a few days of trying to look after the kitten, you realise that you don't want the kitten anymore. You think you are better off with no animals. Either some of them get sick, or some of them die with you looking after them. You ask Shalini to take you to the pet shop again. She takes you, only this time you are embarrassed. You know that the man behind the counter isn't going to be happy. You say, "Sorry Mr, I came back to leave this kitten, my parents don't want me to keep it."

He looks at you and Shalini silently for a second. He says, "Ok see that door over there." You look to where he's pointing. You say, "Yes." He says, "Go through there and leave the kitten there." You and Shalini go through there and leave the kitten there. You wonder if this means that it's abandoned. The kitten tries following you, but you move it out of the way before closing the door behind you. You get your money back, and think this is probably best for you and them.

Months go by, and you missed having animals but realise it's probably better this way. You find out from Shalini that the pet shop called home just after your last visit there. Shalini tells you that they said, "Saesha can't buy anymore animals from us. She keeps coming here to swap her animals over. Animals have feelings too."

Abhay works part time in a shop in Johannesburg and around this time, December, he works full time. Often that is the time shops need more staff, with Christmas being around the corner. Abhay is home some evenings at six or seven.

One day while walking you find a black bird on the street. It has a damaged wing. You decide to take it home. You find a box, and put some food and water inside. You decide to leave it in the house; since it could be killed outside at night, especially if it can't fly. You really don't know how to look after its wing, you can't see a wound on it's wing, and all you can see is that it can't move it very well. You think well at least it can rest, and that way it can get better.

Abhay comes home and switches the television on. As he watches T.V in the dark, he hears a sound. He turns his head to where the sound came from and sees a bird standing on the edge of the box. He screams out loud, "Who brought a bird in the house?" You come running, to see if the bird is ok. You are surprised to find, that it managed to get out of such a high box. This means that at least it can fly a bit. You put the bird back in the box, but it soon becomes impossible because it keeps jumping out the whole time.

The next evening you want to see if it's ok to fly now. You take the box outside, and off it goes. It flies as if it never had an injury. A few days after you find another bird in the driveway. It catches your attention because you see it moving on the ground trying to defend itself from the red ants, that are trying to eat it alive. It seems like a car knocked it down. You take a tissue and push the red ants out of its eye and body. They cling onto the poor bird with their teeth. It makes you so angry, because you can see the injured bird suffering. You manage to pull them off the bird, and quickly take the bird to the back yard. You put some water in your hand and make him drink. Your mum watches, and then the bird dies. You feel so bad when it dies. Your mum says, "Saesha never mind, at least you gave him some water to drink before he died." Another day you find a pigeon as you come from Gujarati school. You pick it up and came running home. Shalini says, "It's dead Saesha, its neck moves like that whether it's dead or alive." In the end, she was right.

Standard Four

In Standard four you feel like Vivek is stealing all your friends. He often hangs out with the two sisters who hang around with you. You've been hanging around with them for some time now. Their names are Chameli and Juhi. Chameli and Juhi in Sanskrit means "Jasmine" as in the flower. In looks and some character, they are both one and the same. They don't have such a big age gap, and look the same age. They are inseparable, and sometimes even match at dressing. They seem like twins. You see some pictures of their mother in black and white, which stands on the TV stand. She looks like a bollywood actress, or a model. It's really easy to guess that she's their mum, because their hair seems like hers; long, soft, shiny and silky. Their faces are oval like hers, both fair, smooth, soft, clear. Their eyes are big, like long thin almonds. They have their dad's eyes and height, hazel brown eyes and tall. You can see why they have different names, which means the same thing. They often go with a big group to the cinema on the last day of school, before everyone goes on school holidays. They do this often during this year.

The first time you find out that they're all going to the cinema together, is through them. You feel completely left out. Friends of Vivek's that have sisters younger than you even get to go along. They often do things together as a group on school holidays. You often visit the two sisters during the holidays, sometimes Shalini even comes with you. You can't understand why you are left out of all their outings. You think perhaps it isn't Chameli and Juhi who leaves you out, it's probably Vivek. He often doesn't want you to go where he goes, he doesn't like you hanging around his friends, yet some friends from the group he hangs out with have more common things with you, and are even in the same class or standard as you. So many people you made friends with first, end up in his group in the end.

The more they go out the more angry you get with Chameli and Juhi. You wonder, "If I am real friends with Chameli and Juhi, than why don't they insist on me coming with them?" They often go to Pitu's house to swim. Pitu lives a few houses away. His friends call him "Peter." Pitu in Sanksrit means "sun and fire." One day, Pitu's father takes all his kids and Vivek to the cinema. You are standing outside the house just as they leave their driveway. Vivek calls you for something and you go running. You want to go with them, and Pitu's father asks you if you want to come. He says, "You can be Pitu's girlfriend." You get shy and say no because you know that your brother doesn't want you around. Pitu has thick light brown eyebrows, eyes and light brown hair. His mother's hair is like his, like white people. It's common to use the term white, and black. Everyone around you uses it, nobody ever says, "Caucasian", or "African."

Often everyone calls Pitu, "Peter," you don't know why, and almost everyone that knows him on the street calls him "Peter." The first thing people do is sing when they hear the name Peter, they'll sing, "Peter Peter pumpkin eater." That's what comes to everyone's mind. It's a nursery rhyme that you all learnt when you were all younger.

During the holidays, you ask your sister to come with you to the park, but she's always with your mother. Juhi and Chameli call you whenever it interests them. You are still so childish and make stupid jokes, which they laugh at. Somedays you feel like you are their form of entertainment. Sometimes you go to their house when you see them through the window or when you want someone to hang out with. At times when you go over to their house they won't open the door for you. You try to be more mature, but it doesn't help. People get used to your soft character; it's easy to push you around. Your problem is that when you are angry you never have the guts to say anything to people. You are afraid to say something and don't want to be the bad one. Even if you want to say something, it never comes out, and if it does come out, it never comes out right, so people laugh right at you; in your face. Sometimes you overthink things and try studying your thoughts so that they can come out right, but it never works. You try talking to Shalini about it, saying that mainly it happens with your friends and with people at school, but she finds it funny and laughs about it.

One day you tell yourself, "Saesha it's you who is weird, it's only happening to you. Shalini doesn't have and never had the same problems you're having." You stop confiding in Shalini, you are often quiet and say only what's necessary. You start bottling up things inside. Sometimes you are so bored that even the boredom beats your anger, and that returning to the little friendship you have with Chameli and Juhi is better than having no friends. You have no cinema in the area, no mall, not much for young people to do here. Everything needs a car. That's why on the last day of school, or somedays during the holidays Vivek and his friends get together and go to the cinema in Johannesburg. If you want to go to the cinema, you had no one to go with in the first place, and secondly don't know how to get there.

At a hall two blocks from your street, there is a film night on Sundays, where you sometimes go and see a Bollywood film. It's where you go to Gujarati school; also it's a venue for weddings and other Hindu events. You imagine the cinema to be just like the hall you go to somedays, to watch Bollywood films. It's where rich people of the same cast get married. Often the biggest weddings of the same cast in town take place there. The name of the hall is called "The Hindu Samaj." Samaj means society or a place of worship. "The Hindu Samaj" even has some concerts where random boys and girls your age gather to practise dances, which often is like the more modern Bollywood dancing. You want to learn to dance like the women in the Bollywood films and want to join an Indian classical dance school.

As you watch Bollywood films, your father points in a direction and says, "Watch how they do it in the film, and dance over there, in that corner." You go to the corner and try it out, but feel pretty stupid and stop. You give up trying since all the pretty light skinned girls get together and form a dance group. You realize that you have to be light skinned and pretty to be able to have luck in this culture. All the pretty, light skinned girls get picked most of the time when it comes to school concerts.

You now reaching a moment where you begin to dislike

your culture. You ask yourself frequently, "Why must I learn this stupid language? Why is it so important that I learn this language? Why is it so important to learn how to cook and clean at such a young age? Why is it so important to be like other Indian girls when I don't even fit in? "Why is being light skinned so important?"

One weekend during your holidays, you, Vivek, and Shalini accompany your parents to Dharti Kaka's house. Your little cousin who once annoyed you when you stayed over with them seems to have changed. You can't wait for Dharti Kaka to ask, "You want to stay over?" You know he's going to ask you eventually. He says the magic words. At first you pretend that you don't want to and than get a little bit of convincing from your cousins and your uncle. You say to your little cousin, "Oh! Ok, I'll stay over." You don't have clothes, but you and Vivek did this once. Your cousins say, "You can wear some of our clothes," but know that the next day, your parents will send your clothes with someone nearby who works near Dharti Kaka.

Your mother says, "We'll send the clothes with Bhai." She calls Bhai the man who they often send your clothes with. Bhai, is a general word that shows respect to a man in the Hindu culture. It also means brother. So the problem's solved, they are going to pick you up in a week and you'll have your clothes tomorrow.

The next day you wake up early, you wake up with a smile on your face. You hear your name. Your aunty asks your grandma, "Did you say something to Lalita Ben?" Lalita was the incarnation of Goddess Durga in Hindu Mythology. Lalita in Sanskrit means playful, charming, desirable, lovely and gentle. "Durga" the Sanskrit word means "invincible." Lalita is your mum's name. You start to pay careful attention when you hear your mum's name. Your granny says, "No I didn't say anything, why?" Your aunty says, "Lalita Ben sounds angry she said Saesha must come home today with the Bhai that works near us." It's your first time staying alone without your siblings. You haven't even spent one day here and you have to head back tonight. You think something big must have gone down and are bothered and think that perhaps something has happened to your father, brothers or sister. You get out of bed when you hear your aunty say, "I'm going to call Lalita Ben, and see what happened." Your aunty is calling from the phone in the kitchen, and the kitchen is just in front of where you are. You hear your aunty pressing the buttons. You pray and hope that everything is ok at home. You wait for someone to speak. Your aunty says, "Hello, Lalita Ben." It sounds like your mum knows who it is. "Pity I can't hear what mum's saying," you wonder. Your aunty says, "Let her stay for somedays." You can't hear more but know that the call is finished. You have to get up, since you hear your cousins. You get out of the room, and don't know what to do. It's uncomfortable. Your aunty doesn't say anything. The day is going by, and by now, your clothes should have been here. You don't have a nice day, because you are disturbed about the call and wonder what could have happened at home.

The next day you wake up with some arguments. It's about you and now you just don't want to come out of the bed and this room ever again. You don't even want to go home. You believe this situation can be handled

71

better. You feel like a problem here now. You still don't know what everything was about. They are on the phone for so long that things seem out of hand. Your aunty is upset and angry and you don't know how your mother is. You can't handle more, and say to your aunty, "It's better I go home, it's better for everyone." She says, "It's your decision whether you want to stay or not." You can't believe you are still given that option. You don't expect an option. You suggested it in case your aunty and uncle didn't know how to tell you. You want to make it easier for them.

It's now the second night. Your mum calls and wants to speak to you. She's talking non- stop and you don't know what's happening. She's making your head spin. Your uncle communicates using actions asking you, "What is she saying?" You are really angry with your mum. You really hate her for the way she's handling this. You take the phone away from your ear, because it's too much. You don't say a word yet and all this is being dumped on top of you. You don't even know what happened. She's talking about a whole lot of things that don't make sense to you.

Your aunty brings a recorder and quickly puts it to the phone. It's already on rec and play. You know this isn't right, and right now you hate your mother alot. She tells you to come home but you just don't know how to do it, "How, I don't even know where to go to go home?" You are uncomfortable with not having your own clothes. Your borrow your cousins.

The first day, you use the same clothes but now you really aren't comfortable. Your cousins lend you some clothes. Your aunty could only hear a little of what was recorded on the phone. You feel so uncomfortable around your cousins. You spend one last day with your cousins. For you this is it, the end. You won't go and stay with any family again after the way your mother behaved, and now no one will want you to stay with them. In everyones' eyes, you are a problem even in your own eyes you feel like one. You don't want to ever speak to your mum again. You want to leave and run away from home forever.

You return home with the man who usually brings your clothes when you and your siblings stayed over at Dharti Kakas' house. You are nervous about getting home. On the way home you wonder, "Whats' going to happen to me? Am I going to get a hiding?" Luckily, you will be home the time your dad returns. You get home and there's silence. After seeing this side of your mother these last few days, you really hate her. You wonder and are almost sure that Abhay, Vivek and Shalini, are going to be mad at you, and blame you for everything that happened during these days. Shalini says, "You caused so many problems, why did you have to go and stay without any clothes?" It surprises you that your brothers don't say anything to you. You tell Shalini, "You were there; they seemed fine about me staying over." You ask her, "What happened here? I don't get it!" Your sister says, "Mum wanted to leave your clothes with that Bhai and Papa also wanted to go and leave your clothes," than they fought about who's going to leave the clothes. After that, your mum ignores you more, and that isn't a surprise. She ignored you before anyway.

One day you are with Chameli and Juhi, and your mum and sister are going somewhere. You ask them, "Can I come with you?" You don't feel like hanging out with Chameli and Juhi. Your mum says, "No, you can't come with us!" You ask that question to your sister again, because your mum always says no when you want to hang out with them. Your mum repeats, "No!" You have enough; you tell your mum in front of Chameli and Juhi, "I'm going to run away from home." You want to say more to your mum, but have to hold it in. You stop yourself from saying personal stuff in front of your friends.

You have no relationship with your mother, or your father. Your father has always been the same, but from the beginning, you have no connection with your mother. Sometimes you ask yourself, "Just why was I bought into this world? This is not a normal family." Your mother acts as if you don't exist.

Your mum and dad don't do anything together. Your father doesn't speak to her with respect. They sleep in separate beds. Aunties and uncles used to tell you and your siblings to push their beds together, but you have always seen it this way, and never understand why they said what they said. The fact that your parents never sleep in the same bed seems normal to you, you've seen them sleeping in separate beds always. Abhay never joins any family gatherings anymore, and you all never eat together.

After leaving school, Abhay stopped going to any family gatherings, and disappears when people come to visit. They always give him a lecture about leaving school. He often goes out at night and comes home late. Your dad doesn't like him coming home late. He gives him a curfew, and if he doesn't come home before or at that time, your dad locks him out and puts the door chain on. When that happens Abhay knocks on you and your sister's bedroom window. If the window's a little open he whispers until he wakes one of you up. Shalini often gets the keys from the kitchen and quietly lets him in. Eventually your dad starts sleeping with the keys under the pillow and one morning when you wake up, Shalini takes you to the back window. You see Abhay sleeping with a cardboard box on top of him, which he opened up, and probably got from the yard during the night. You feel sorry for Abhay at times and at other times, he just causes so many problems.

You and Shalini look for Chunks but he isn't there anymore. It's been months since you both saw him. The thought of him being dead is painful and sad. None of you said goodbye to him. Anuj Kaka is moving to America. When you visit them you always play with his dog, he's Chunks brother. He's much more smaller than Chunks. Chunks was huge compared to Bhajiya. "Bhajiya" is the name of the dog. "Bhajiya" is the Gujarati word while some people in India refer to it as "Pakora." Bhajiyas are fritters, made with a spicy chickpea batter; it can include different vegetables, and are deep-fried. They have different shapes, the one you often see in the Gujarati culture are round bhajiyas.

Since Anuj Kaka is moving away, he asks you if you want to keep Bhajiya. You are excited and say yes. Bhajiya has a habit of climbing onto your legs tight, he moves his penis back and forth. No matter how much you move try to get him off your leg he always trys again.

One day your mother goes to a wedding alone at The Hindu Samaj. She sometimes go with Shalini or sometimes go alone. You and Shalini don't join her this time. During pre wedding ceremonies and other Hindu events it's common to find that women allow men, and kids to eat first and then they eat last. In the final wedding ceremonies, men and women eat separately.

Your mother comes home alone, and she seems bothered. You find out that Dharti kaka's wife spilled water on her sari. You know that things are not good between them, and don't know if it was actually a mistake. You think to yourself, "How can the spill hit her straight in the front, making it look like she peed." You see her face, it's sad and broken. There's obviously no proof to say whether it was a mistake or if it was intentional but seeing that today your mum has a face of a woman who has nothing left, her dignity has been ripped out from her heart. You are saddened by the humiliated look your mum has. Your father often does things on his own, he doesn't do a lot of things with your mum, this is something normal for you. It's how you always remember it.

It's Deepavali, in Sanskrit Deepavali means "row of lights." Deepavali or Diwali as Gujaratis call it is the most important celebration of the year for Hindus. Just as Christmas is the most important celebration for Christians. Others refer to Diwali as "the festival of lights." Days before Diwali and on Diwali's day Hindus light little clays lamps filled with oil or ghee. "Ghee" is a Sanskrit word, and means clarified butter. These clay lamps are called "Divos," pronounced "Deevau." "Divo" in Gujarati means "lamp." In Sanksrit "Diya" means light. Hindus light many divos in their homes during this festival, which signifies good over evil. It is also common to burst fireworks to drive away evil spirits. You eat both sweet and savoury snacks during Diwali. There is one Muslim family on your road, all the rest are Hindus. On Diwali, they never mix much with others, or just mix with the neighbours. It's the only house in the whole street that isn't lit up.

During Diwali you often go to sleep or watch TV after your fireworks are finished. It is spring and a hot night; often your family leaves the door open, but just close the front door gate. You hear another gate open and run to see who's here from the window; you think it's one of your brothers. To your surprise, you see the father of the house from the Muslim family marching over to the front door, he seems angry and when he arrives to the front door gate, he asks you angrily, "Where is your father?" You try to go and open the gate for him but he already manages to open it himself while you answer his question, "His sleeping," you say. He goes straight to your father's room, which is in front of the kitchen. He pushes the slightly closed door open. That's where your father and mother sleep and says raising his voice loudly, "Put your pants on, and look what your son has done!" Your father quickly gets up to put on his pants. The man makes his way to the salon where you are. Your father doesn't follow the man since he's putting his pants on. Shalini and you run off from the angry man's sight. Your father goes to the salon and doesn't know what to do, or say since he doesn't know what happened. The man says, "Your son lit some fireworks just as some visitors came out of my house. He did it right in front of my door and ran away." "Again, Abhay has to spoil the peace at home," you wonder. Your father says, "I'll speak to him, when he returns." By now, your father is used to getting into trouble because of Abhay.

There are loads of arguments now with Abhay and your father. He goes out a lot and comes home late. Your father tells him, "You have to find a full time job now. It's enough." The tension doesn't seem like it's ever going to end. Your family still don't have a car. You think Abhay is selfish to think about himself. He has friends who have cars and he gets picked up at home for work. You all don't go on picnics and can't do anything without the car. Having a car is important. Your mother and your father have to catch a lift with someone if there are important family events. Sometimes people don't have space for both of them, so one of them has to go. "Abhay didn't just mess up things for himself but he messed up things for all of us. He doesn't even think of mummy and papa," you wonder. Abhay even knows what your mum holds in her account. She has 17 000 Rands. You think, "Wow that's a lot." Abhay asks your mother for the money saying he is going to look after it for her. You know that's not true. You know Abhay will evenually just keep it for himself. Your mother doesn't buy anything for herself, and you don't even know if your father gives her money. You are angry with Abhay and say to yourself, "His a boy and the eldest, and that allows him the right to take over everyone." You also are angry at your mother.

Standard Five

You get to standard five and are surprised to find
Chameli in your class. You already have your friends
and she has hers with whom she hangs around with
during breaktime. Chameli is repeating standard five
again. Over the last few months, you stop hanging
around with her and her sister. Juhi is now in high
school. She goes to a different school. In class, Chameli
sits with the girl who she hangs out with during
breaktime, after school and weekends. Another
neighbour comes and hangs around with you a lot, she
is your age but in another class.

Today Bhajiya is coming. Anuj Kaka is going to
America and he's going to live near Kalpana Masi.
Kalpana Masi moved to America at least three years
ago. Anju Kaka brings his kennel. He tells you what
Bhajiya likes, and you ask, "Does he eat dog food?"
Anuj Kaka says, "No, he always eats what we eat."
Your eyebrows lift up in a funny way, you are not sure
if you heard right. "Bhajiya is vegetarian," you inquire.
Anuj Kaka's family is vegetarian just like your family,
but it isn't normal for you to see a vegetarian dog. "Yes
Bhajiya is vegetarian," says Anuj Kaka. Anuj Kaka and
his family says bye to Bhajiya. Bhajiya looks upset.
Your neighbour is with you. She is excited to see your
dog and you both try to cheer Bhajiya up. You feed
Bhajiya delicious dog food that night to make him
happy. Bhajiya eats his food, it's as if he has never
tasted something so luscious. It's obviously meat. He
eats it so fast.

He eventually gets used to your house. He often goes in

circles chasing his tail. He runs from far and jumps against the wall to see the neighbour's yard. He used to do it a lot at Anuj Kaka's house to see the pool next door. When he realizes that there is no pool next door he stops jumping on the wall.

You never like going to your mum's side of the family when you hear things. One day, Shalini goes to leave something at Devi Masi's house. "Devi" in Sanskrit means "goddess." Devi Masi is on your mother's side of the family. Her husband is the one who came to help your father when Abhay was in an accident with the Toyota Corolla. Her husband's name is Manit, but you and your siblings all call him Manit Kaka. Manit is of Sanskrit origin and means "honoured or respected." They live in a mansion and are a very respected family.

Shalini once went to leave something that your mum gave her at Devi Masi's house. Manit Kaka spoke to Shalini through the window instead of opening the door. He took what your sister gave him from the window. Abhay was given a job by them in the Market. He used to work everyday from four in the afternoon to four in the morning, summer and winter. He used to get paid one thousand rands a month. He only went out in the weekends. Somehow, Abhay started disliking Manit Kaka's family a lot. Manit Kaka's son was almost the same age as Abhay and use to say to Abhay disgustingly, "You smoke marijuana." You don't know whether it was true or false but he always acted superior than your brothers and sister. Abhay used to get put down a lot by family, after leaving school and smashing the car.

Shalini never wants to go to Manit and Devi Masi's house, neither does Vivek, neither does Abhay, and automatically you don't want to go to their house after seeing their reaction. Your mum's side of the family is big and one day during the holidays, your mum takes you to visit someone on her side of the family. Sita Masi is the name of this aunty. Sita means "furrow" in Sanskrit. In Hindu mythology, Sita was the daughter of the goddess of the earth. She was discovered in a furrow. Your mum's side of the family never comes to your house. Your cousins at the family where you are going to visit don't have a big age difference with you. You like them because they are down to earth. They used to be rich until their father's friend betrayed him and stole the business off him. Sita Masi and your cousins ask you to stay over, but you don't want to, not after what happened the last time. Your mum insists a lot and you tell your mum that you don't want to stay over. She keeps insisting that you stay over and so you do. Your cousins are over excited and say, "Come on it's going to be fun." Your mums' side of the family analyzes most things you say, but you just try to avoid answering all their personal questions. Your mum says, "Dad will drop your clothes over tonight." You think it's fine, because you don't live far from them anyway. You rollerskate and do other things with your cousins. You play with the girls especially and are only allowed to be in the house, backyard and only as far as the front yard. Sita Masi has a lot of visitors and you don't even know most of them. She is peeling a bag of peas with some other women, yet you feel as if you have to help too. When you ask to help, you aren't allowed, so you just stop offering to help.

Before the end of the holidays, Sita Masi tells her kids that they must go and see Devi Masi. You don't want to go there, but you have to since they're going. You and your two cousin sisters take a walk to Devi Masi's house. Devi Masi offers you a drink or something to eat. You say no. You feel really uncomfortable; because you can count the number of times you have been there. Devi Masi says, "Why don't you all go and play with the kids outside? They're all playing together?" You don't want to play with all of these rich kids. You don't know them. As you and your cousins leave the door, they start running to the other kids. You walk slowly towards them. They're all playing cricket and you and your cousins are fielders. You think they're going to treat you bad, but after thirty minutes of playing with them you are actually having fun. "They are actually nice, my aunty is actually nice. It doesn't make sense what Abhay and Shalini said," you wonder. Soon the ball comes to your side and you go running for it. You go and fetch the ball, and when you turn around to throw it, all the children are running away from you, they've disappeared. You are angry that the cousins whom you got to know and had fun with fell into their influence. "It's understandable; perhaps they don't want to be the next lot that would go through what I'm going through. Perhaps they came here often and didn't want to lose the people who they often play with or else they'd get the same treatment," you wonder. They expect you to run behind them and look for them, but you are not going to do that. You decide to head home to their house since you are staying there, but luckily, it's your last day and now you have a good reason not to return to their house anymore. You decide to leave; you can't believe that at this age people can still do this to you. You say to yourself, "This is not my place, I am in the wrong place, at least I am not a fake like my cousins, I am poor so what, at least I don't pretend to be rich." You march off and as soon as you are about to leave their premises through the big garden you played in, they all come out of their hiding place. Your cousins come running to you as if nothing happened. You have all of them recorded in your mind. You remember their names and their faces. You swear to yourself that, "This is the first and last time these people will ever get to make a fool out of me!" You go home and that is the end of ever staying over at any families' home. You stopped praying and believing in god a long time ago.

This year is a nice year. At school someone gets nits and lice, so twice a week before entering into the class you all have to get checked by your teacher. After the smelling experience, you changed a lot. You pay more attention to your dressing and hygiene. You know you have no nits and lice. The teacher checks everyone, one by one. It comes to your turn and she says, "I think I saw a nit in your hair." You can't believe it, "It can't be, one nit surely can't be such a big deal," you wonder. When you get home, you ask Shalini to check your hair. She checks and says, "Your hair is clean." You don't believe her, because if the teacher says that, then in two days time she might say you still have it. This won't be good for you and your reputation. You wash your hair at least three times; and even put loads of air freshener on your hair because you don't have perfume. You think, "What ever the teacher saw surely didn't live through what I just put it through." When the teacher rechecks all of you, she tells you, "Your hair is clean." It is a relief to hear her say that, you are okay to enter

83

the class. Days after Chameli and her friend, Hasini
avoids you. Mostly Hasini moves away quickly from
you. In Physical Education, if she just happens to be
next to you or anywhere near you than she'll move
away from you as if you have a disease or something. It
is really uncomfortable when she does that, but finally
she got over it.

You clean Bhajia's mess when you can. Bhajia has a
poop scoop that Anuj Kaka left you with before he went
to America. You clean Bhajia's mess when you can,
and sometimes Shalini and your father helps clean up
Bhajias's poop. Bhajia has a habit of messing in one
part of the garden, just like he did at Anuj Kaka's
house. Your father often puts the poop scoop in a
bucket with hot water. He soaks it in there with some
cleaning liquid. It's a hot summer's day. During
summer, your garden has lots of red ants and solidier
ants around. They make their colonies in the outside
floor. The flooring is old and often ants bite your mum
when she hangs the clothes on the washing line. They
come out from small holes from the outside floor. Your
mum often puts salt in the area where she hangs the
clothes so that the ants would stay away. During the hot
summers night soldier ants often come out of their
colonies. Sometimes it's impossible to sit on the grass
in the front yard, or even stand there. The ants even fill
the walkway between the outside and inside gate. You
have to open two gates before entering the porch.

One weekend Abhay and his friend Mitrá decide to
hang out. Mitrá in Sanskrit means "friend". Mitrá
comes sometimes to hang out with Abhay. You are
inside the house. When Abhay comes with his friends,

84

you go and see who's arrived. It's boring when no one is around. Shalini helps your mum and you always look for something to do. Abhay and his friends always seem to do fun stuff. Abhay has a bottle of methylated spirits in his hand, and Mitrá has a box of matches. You ask, "What's that for?" Abhay says, "We are going to pour the spirits into the holes of the ants and set it alight. We are going to burn all the ants." You think, "Wow that sounds like some nice fireworks display." You imagine the ants running around while they're on fire, and want to watch but Abhay doesn't want you around. As soon as you make your way into the house you re-think the plan, "It's not a good idea to kill them like that, they are going to suffer. If they kill them, they are going to end up paying for that deed in their life. It's better to not do any harm to them and that throwing salt is much more harmless," you wonder. After thinking that through you wonder, "Watching something die and suffer isn't cool anymore." You go inside and manage to keep yourself busy.

At least thirty minutes go by when you hear a small scream. It sounds like Mitrá, but then a few seconds after your mum screams something like, "Aye! Aye!" You run so fast, open the kitchen gate and head straight to her in a second. You see Mitrá banging his head against the wall, and your mum is screaming something in Gujarati, which sounds like, "Elok né khai tiyu!" that means "something happened to them!" She is screaming, "Help! Somebody help!" You run to Mitrá, he is the first in your sight. You see a flame around his head. Your mum goes looking for Abhay. The first thing you find is the water where Bhajia's poop scoop is soaked. The water has pieces of poop. You say, "It's

85

a matter of life and death." You take the poop scoop out, pick up the bucket and go running to Mitrá. Mitrá sees it, and grabs it from your hand and throws the water on top of him, for a second he has the bucket dangling over his head. He pulls it off. You turn around worried looking to see if Abhay is okay. You're thinking the worst. Your mum is dragging him to where she was washing the clothes, and puts his face in the water. He's been burning longer than Mitrá yet doesn't even scream. The neighbour is already looking over the wall. She came out after hearing your mum screaming and wants to see if everything is ok. Someone already called the ambulance, and as Mitrá and Abhay wait for the ambulance, you see how sad and worried they are about their burns. Someone asks them what happened, and Abhay says, "We were trying to burn the ants, when the methylated spirits fell over." The ambulance takes them to the hospital. Your father comes home early, because he had to be at the hospital. Mitrá's family is notified about what happened. When your father comes back from the hospital he says, "Abhay has a third degree burn, while Mitrá has a second-degree burn. The doctor says that it's possible that Abhay's scars won't disappear but Mitrá's would. It's possible that Abhay will need to have plastic surgery done. The next day you and your family finally visit Abhay during visiting hours. Other family members found out what happened and are here to visit Abhay at the hospital too. You all worry so much, and when you see Abhay, he has a bandage all over his face. Mitrá was released from hospital. Abhay looks really very sad. Some of your cousins who stand with your uncles are there too. As you come out of the room from visiting Abhay, you overhear some of your cousins, criticising and laughing at what Abhay did when he got burnt. You are offended and furious, "Why did they come to see him? Or did they just come to see the show? This isn't a place to criticise someone for their actions, besides, he's lying in hospital right now." When Abhay comes home, you feel sorry for him. He is always using products that he thinks is helping him heal his skin. He is troubled that he's going to look like this all his life. Mitrá comes to visit Abhay, his scars are already gone. As time goes by Mitrá hardly comes to your house.

You don't want to continue going to The Hindu Samaj, where you have Gujarati classes. You have only two more years left to finish Gujarati school forever. You are a little tired of it and are looking for a way to end it off for once and for all but don't know how Vivek, Shalini, and Abhay dropped out. You are so sick of it that you don't see the point of reaching so high in the Gujarati and Hindi language when at the end you aren't going to do anything with it. You think it's a complete waste of time, and just hate the language. Even if you can speak well, you are embarrased to speak it. You pretend as if you hardly know anything and make it a point to answer in English. You are sick of the fact that you have to act and do things in a certain way, as Indian people and women should. Up to now, learning this doesn't make you any less or more of a Gujarati. You think of a plan. In your house there is no communication, therefore it is hard for you to communicate this. You ask your father if you can change schools. You don't have a problem with the school where you go, but insist that you want to change. You have a plan. Exhaustingly you wonder, "What a long way to get rid of going to school."

You start to get other ideas. You think, "Perhaps it isn't a bad idea changing schools, you might even be popular in the other school." You are very good at Gujarati, and do some Hindi in The Hindu Samaj.

You change schools, and go to the school were Chameli and Hasini go to, you know you were better off at studying Gujarati at The Hindu Samaj. Your old school is more professional. You become a little popular but lose interest in Gujarati completely. An important exam is coming up, you know you can pass it easily but decide not to study for the Gujarati exams. Hasini sits next to you in the exam. She tries to peek on your page for answers, but when she sees that you have all the wrong answers she wants you to copy from her. You just don't care, and don't want to. You lose complete interest for Gujarati.

You now want to be kicked out of Gujarati school and decide not to go to school and go to the park. The park is right in front of Gujarati school. You decide to disappear for a few days so that you can get kicked out. It's really boring going to the park; it takes so much effort to do this. "It's actually better to pass hours at home than at a boring park," you wonder desperately.

The next day, after English school, your mother tells you strictly, "Why aren't you going to Gujarati school?" You see Abhay, your father and Vivek talking to her rudely and take the courage to tell her rudely too, "I'm not going to Gujarati school, you can't force me." "I'm going to give you a hiding, you're going to school today," she says angrily. She's coming for you, and you run away and leave the house saying, "I'm not going there anymore." You come back in the evening when your father returns. It looks like she's not angry anymore. Your father doesn't know that you took it upon yourself not to return to Gujarati school. Your mum and dad don't talk about it, and he never asks about it. You wonder, how did she find out that you're dodging Gujarati school. You never see your mum push you this bad, over Gujarati school. Strange enough she never says anything after that. You look back and wonder, "It seemed important to her for me to continue with Gujarati. I didn't know how important it was for her until that day." "Aaaah, now I have my afternoons free, finally," you tell yourself stretching your legs out on the table today. You look at the clock and breath in cooly, it's the usual time you had to go to Gujarati school. You still feel guilty for putting your mum through that. You have the rememberance of her face, she just seemed so crushed, when you told her you didn't want to go to Gujarati school anymore.

So a few months go by and amazingly enough Abhay's scars are hardly visible. He doesn't need to have plastic surgery after all. Abhay has a friend who has a car. They hang out at your house almost everyday. Abhay and this friend are good friends for a while. In fact the day the Toyota got smashed Abhay was dropping off his friend who didn't live very far from the corner where Abhay had met up in an accident. You and Shalini always splash Abhay's friend with water. He always hangs out at your house. When you and Shalini start the water fights it never ends, everyone is eventually involved. It helps on really hot summer days.

89

Your school friends come sometimes to hang out with you all and sometimes Abhay's friend takes all of you for a drive. During school holidays, Chameli and Juhi often hang around at their grandparents place. Chameli and her sister also comes around when Abhay's friend comes to your house. You find out that Chameli likes Abhay's friend.

One day Chameli and Juhi call you to their house. They aren't at their grandparent's house but at their other house. You go over to theirs since it's not far from yours. When you get there, Juhi opens the door. You come in and don't see Chameli around. Juhi says, "Come to the room." You follow and when you get there, you find Hasini there. You aren't surprised, because Chameli and Hasini stick together like glue. Chameli is on the phone and Hasini is listening closely. They are speaking to a boy.

That day you find out that he's a friend of your brother's. A guy who is studying law. He isn't the friend who comes to your house often, but another one in the group. They find his number, and get his surname from the times they hang around with you. You are surprised, "How many more are they doing this to?" You are actually disgusted. This friend of Abhay's is really nice to you. They have already been doing this for over a month, calling him and pretending to be a secret admirer. That day it's too late for you to warn him. He is coming to the park, which is in front of Chameli and Juhi's house that very day. Apparently, he's going to meet his secret admirer that day. They wait and peep through the window to look out for his car. As soon as he arrives, he waits right in the centre of the park facing Chameli and Juhi's house. You sigh with relief, "At least Juhi is innocent," you wonder until she takes out the binoculars. She moves the curtain a little and exclaims, "Guys check this!" Chameli pulls the binoculars from her, looks, and says "Oh! My god he came with a rose." They laugh about how they fooled him, and expect you to laugh with them. You pretend and go along with them to find out what more they have done, and to whom. He's still waiting there, and you really want to go out and let him know what's going on.

As time goes by they disgust you. They spy on their cousin who comes to the park with her boyfriend, and use the binoculars to see exactly what they are up to. Hasini and Chameli laugh as they make people believe that they are in some kind of a competition, and make people roar on the phone to win the competition. They even call some houses, and depending on the tone of the voice, they judge if it's a woman or a man. They say, "Your husband is cheating on you." You don't find this funny at all.

You want to tell your brother's friend what they are doing. When you see him, you try telling him, but not everything comes out. He says disappointingly, "How can you do this to me? Leave those friends, they're bad for you!" Abhay's friend hardly comes around but the one who Shalini and you used to wet on hot summer days still comes around. You consider keeping your distance with Chameli and Juhi, but it's too difficult. When you don't want to go to theirs, they come looking for you at yours.

It's Diwali again, Shalini and your mum usually make the divos. Other houses on the street have some very original things. There's a house covered with creepers and climbers. There the people usually put divos in small bottles and hang them onto the creepers and climbers in certain areas of the garden. The house looks very beautiful with dangling oil lamps. The oil lamps last for hours that way, without the wind blowing it off. You always see some peacocks in their garden. The peacocks were bought after the temple was built. At first, they used to stay within the temple grounds and then started moving out into the neighbourhood. Diwali always ends early for you. You don't have anything to do after you finish your fireworks. Shalini and you try to keep the divos alive for longer, but it soon becomes boring. Juhi and Chameli always celebrate Diwali for few hours at their grandparents place and then go to their other house.

This Diwali Juhi and Chameli stay for longer, so you go to hang out with them. It's around half past eleven, and they too seem bored. You see Vivek and his friends from where you're standing. They made a big fire with some boxes they've found on the street close to Pitu's house. Vivek's group calls Juhi, Chameli and you to join them. You don't care less about what Vivek thinks and go with Juhi and Chameli. They all decide to collect empty, burst fireworks shells. They have a plan, and so you all hunt for the shells of flares, rockets, wheels and other shells, which are big and visible. You all line up the street, from where the road starts; in front of your house right across to were the street ends; the opposite neighbour. You all put the big shells starting in the centre of the street to small going outwards. One

92

boy from Vivek's group has some loose Tom Thumbs crackers that he finds on the street while looking for fireworks shells. It's common to find unburst Tom Thumbs on the streets during this time of the year. Once the line is finished, you all hide away when you all see a car coming in your direction. The person who has the Tom Thumbs quickly takes one loose cracker from the string and puts it on the biggest shell, which stands in the centre of the road. As the cars come in the direction of the empty shells they usually stop when the driver sees something alight. Sometimes the Tom Thumb bursts just when the car stops. That's usually the plan. The driver waits for a bit, presuming that one of the fireworks or sometimes the whole line is alight. You all chuckle without making a big noise, hiding behind the wall while one person peeps from the side of the gate reporting what the driver is up to, to the rest of you. Sometimes the driver doesn't dare to run over the fireworks just in case something is alight, and passes from the side of the road running over the smaller shells. One driver even stops in front of the line and goes right through it, running over the bigger shells. You usually have a lot of fun with Vivek's friends. They never tease you, and treat you the same as they treat others in the group, yet you still can't understand why Vivek has a problem with you hanging out with them. "If Chameli, Juhi, girls that I am friends with at school, and other sisters of the boys in the group can hang out with them than why can't I?," you wonder.

This school year is fun; the school makes a trip to Drakensburg. All the Standard Five classes go along; those kids who want to go, or who's allowed to go by their parents. You have fun, and get along with everyone. There are no embarrassing moments, and everything goes smooth and pleasant. Your classmates are nice to you; after all, it is the last year before you all end up going to high school, and you make the best of it, in fact it seems like you all make the best of it.

Now that exams are over and you all still have to be in class for somedays, you do some fun things. For English you have to do show and tell. Show and tell is about bringing something and showing the class how it's done, or made. You have less then thirty minutes to show the class with samples. You can do it in pairs or groups. You don't have anyone to do it with. Chameli and Hasini decide to work together. No one asks you to join their group, so you're thinking of things you can do on your own. You're trying to think about interesting things to do. One person brings silk worms and you enjoy seeing show and tell on silk worms. You didn't know a creature this beautiful even exists. The fact that this beautiful creature makes a silk cocoon is pretty impressive. After that, you too want to do something nice and impressive too. You still have time to prepare your idea. You think of a cat or a dog, but since you don't have one, it isn't possible.

One day you go with Chameli and Juhi to the petshop. You see a kitten that you like and consider buying one just for show and tell, but it isn't a good idea. You don't want to handle the problem of having a kitten when you have Bhajia around. Chameli falls in love with the kitten. It's soon going to be Chameli and Hasina's turn to do show and tell. Chameli and Hasini come in with the kitten that you liked from the pet shop for show and tell. Everyone is dying to touch it. No one up to now brought something so big and alive for show and tell. It's breaktime and after break Chameli and Hasini are going to do the show and tell on cats. You decide to head to your class just before breaktime ends. The classroom door is shut, which is quite strange. When you open it, you find some classmates inside. You get in, and they scream, "Shut the door behind you!" Hasini and Chameli are there too, they're busy looking for the kitten. The kitten is out of the cage and running loose all over the class, it's hard to get hold of it, but finally they manage it.

Soon it's going to be your turn to do show and tell. You're excited and find a nice idea. Shalini takes you to a friend who did something for show and tell a few years ago. She gives you a good idea. Shalini's friend often made chocolates and used moulds to shape them for different occasions. She makes chocolate arrangements, and chocolates which she sells at school for Valentines Day, and other special occasions. She explains and shows you how to make them and tells you what to buy. You buy chocolate moulds, gold dust, and multicoloured aluminium foil. You think of making it more interesting by having a chocolate arrangement to give your class ideas for making their own presents in the future, but think it's too much work. At home, you melt the chocolate as she suggested and pour it into the moulds. You put the moulds in the fridge and wait for it to cool down. Once they cool down, you take them out of the moulds and brush edible gold dust to make the chocolate look elegant. You wrap some in a multicoloured aluminium foil, some with gold dust and some without to show the class how to make the chocolate look elegant.

When you take your show and tell, you explain the process of melting the chocolate and show the class the moulds one can use. You tell them where to buy the moulds and show them what the container of gold dust looks like, and brush it onto the chocolates you made at home to show the class how elegant it makes a chocolate look. After you do your show and tell, you wait for the class to ask you questions, luckily, no one asks you any.

Pitu likes a girl in your class. He seems absolutely in embarrassinglove. Your class teacher picks a few girls to do the end of year concert. Unbelievably, she picks you along with your friends. Even the girl Pitu likes is in the group. Your class teacher decides to show you all some steps as you are going to do an Indian dance. You all get together and practise. Once you are all ready you have to get onto the stage at The Hindu Samaj where the concert will be held to rehearse. You expect loads of people to be there for the rehearsals and are nervous.

It's time for you and the group to meet at The Hindu Samaj. There they already have some costumes. Your teacher isn't going to be there. You meet with the group and go to the hall together. As you all get into the hall with the group, someone runs to the backstage looking for the costumes. She screams, "Here are the costumes!" Everyone runs while you walk onto the stage, you are a little confused and are the last to get onto the stage. They already start putting their costumes on.

Vivek and his group of friends walk in, they sit in the empty seats where the audience normally sit. You get even more nervous, because they're watching. Some of the girls you are with in the group hang around with them. You go and look for a decent costume from what's left. There isn't much of a choice. The costume you find doesn't have a string threaded into it, which you can tie around your waist, the string is separate from the costume. You think the costume is very ugly, and so do the other girls. You all get into position. It's a typical Indian outfit, but really very ugly. The "Odhni" is long enough to put around your waist and over your shoulders. "Odhni" is like a really long silky scarf with embroidery. Some "Odhni's" have rich embroidery and others not. Now you are all are in position, and you pray that nothing is going to happen here to make you look like a fool. You already know the steps, but the fact that your brother and his friends are watching make you lose confidence. You think they're probably saying ugly things about you. The music starts playing and seconds before starting the dance your skirt falls down. You are in shock. You look down at your skirt, than straight ahead at your brother and his friends, down again at your skirt and quickly pull it up and go running behind the curtains. Everyone that saw that are laughing. The girl who is leading everything is angry, and is wondering what happened. She starts to shout, and you say, "Just give me a moment, I'll be there shortly." The other girls tell her, "Saesha's skirt fell down that's why she ran away."

Tying the string around the skirt doesn't help, at the end you are so skinny that even the skirt slides down from under the string. It takes you a while to sort out the skirt properly and then you come out. You do the rehearsal well, but the fact that you feel embarrassed doesn't

97

disappear. You think, "What if they saw my underwear, or bottom!" Luckily, some people from Vivek's group say, "We couldn't see anything because the odhni was in the way." You are saved, but when you go home, Vivek doesn't stop teasing you, and say, "They all saw your panties today aha ha ha." Vivek is always like this. He always make things sound dirtier than they really are.

Your grandma comes to stay over for a few days. She is your father's mother and likes Shalini a lot. To her Shalini is a true Gujarati girl. She always says in Gujarati something, which sounds like this, "Shalini bau dai pauri ché," which means, "Shalini is a good girl." One day your dad slaps your mother in front of your grandmother. You see everything and you can't understand what your mum did to deserve that. Your mum is shocked, and so are you. She doesn't do anything, or say anything, walks with her head down and continues doing what she was doing before being slapped. Your grandmother is in shock and says to your father in Gujarati something like, "Lalita ne khem maré?" Which means, "Why do you hit Lalita?" Abhay never listens to your mother and neither does Vivek. Abhay answers her back, and the fact that Abhay does what he wants, makes you do the same. You too want to do what you want. Girls have to obey, and as a girl you think, "Why does Abhay get to do what he wants? Is it because he is a boy? Well, I too will do what I want!"

Shalini doesn't ever go against your mother or your father. She hangs out with your grandmother a lot, whereas you just want to go and play with the skateboard at times. Hanging out with your grandmother is boring after a while. Shalini never does fun stuff with you and is always in the kitchen. Your grandma thinks that you should be helping in the kitchen instead of playing outside, but Abhay and Vivek are out all day, and you only see them at home in the evenings. When you are bored, you play with all the abandoned stuff that Abhay and Vivek stop playing with. You play with the football, head the ball, and tap the ball on your feet for a good while keeping it from hitting the ground. You learn tricks by yourself after spending so much time with the football. You saw Abhay do it and tried doing it like him. You learn how to use Abhay's skateboard on your own, and start doing tricks with it. One of the tricks you master is going with speed and flipping the skateboard in the air than landing on it with both of your feet. You saw Abhay trying to master the same trick you just mastered and want to show him. You make so much noise with the skateboard that your mum can't even take an afternoon nap with the noise. You go in circles around the house, draw stop signs, and make speed limits with chalk, as if it's a kind of road around the house and than one day you just can't find the skateboard anymore. It just disappears out of the blue.

Abhay does two really cool things. He knows how to use the nunchucks like the one Bruce Lee uses. You and him just call it sticks. The nunchucks that Abhay has are two wooden sticks with a metal chain in between that allows flexible movement while fighting. You only learn how to swing it left to right spinning it over and around your hands but Abhay uses it in such a modern way without doing any Kung Fu tricks. Abhay is also good at using a long stick to fight, you haven't seen anything like it, it looks pretty cool. For some reason he doesn't show people what he knows, it's as if it's embarrassing for him to be good at something. You too find it embarrassing going with the skateboard on the road trying to learn more tricks. You don't see girls playing with skateboards and are afraid of what people might say.

Now it's close to the end of the year concert. Your mum seems so proud of you. You tell her you are going to be in a concert and need a nice Chaniya Choli. A Chaniya is a long heavily embroidered skirt, it's umbrella shaped. The Choli is a blouse that is very short and ends before the waistline. It has a long Odhni too. There are different types of Chaniya Choli's. Chaniya Cholis can be made with cotton, silk, or other types of material. Your mum finds a really nice pretty Chaniya Choli, it's blue and white, made of cotton and has a lot of sequins, mirror work, embroidery, and thread work. She shows it to you and you like it yet it seems a little old. She says, "I'm going to wash it really nice and you'll see how it will glow on the stage." Your mum usually washes everything by hand, your house doesn't have a washing machine.

Soon you are going to get your exam results. Even though you know you passed Standard Five you still have the fear of the unknown. You think to yourself, "What if I am wrong to think that I'm going to pass?" Finally, you are relieved with the results, now you are going to high school. You are ready for the school concert. Your outfit is beautiful. You can't believe you look so nice. Your mum and dad are coming to the concert. You are nervous on stage and with the concert but just thinking about the time you tripped on the stage when getting the prize for the best handwriting makes you scared, however by just looking at yourself today you have so much confidence. You feel as if you are glowing on stage when the curtains open, the multicouloured lights shining on you and your group. Looking at how big the hall is, and the amount of people there is a shock. "I better not embarrass myself," you wonder. The music starts playing and you do all the steps right. At one point, your toe gets stuck into a seam, while you're jumping doing one step. You think you might fall but you can't stop to get it out. You think of forcing your toe out of the seam but are afraid that your skirt might not be able to take it and go back to the day where everyone was laughing at you when your skirt fell down during rehearsals. You think if you do force your toe out this time the skirt could take it because you told your mum to tie the string tight. You finally decide to force the landing on both your feet for the next step. While doing the step you pray that, you don't make a fool out of yourself. You wonder, "Just imagine how embarrassing it could be to mess this up in front of thousands of parents and students!", but luckily, it slides out of the seam just in time to land on both feet. Your mum is so proud of you, she says, "You looked so pretty on stage!" She hardly ever gives compliments so you really appreciate it. Standard Five is the best year of all your primary school life!

It's school holidays. Juhi and Chameli often come to their grandparent's house. Sometimes you find Hasini there; and sometimes Shalini comes with you to hang out with them. Juhi and Chameli have MTV. It's the first time you discover that there are other ways to listen to English music than just plain old radio. You don't know that there is a channel for music. Chameli and Juhi have magazines with the song lyrics too. On MTV, there are some songs that you remember hearing Abhay listening to. At home, you are mostly surrounded by Hindi music, and hardly listen to English music. When Abhay comes home, he gets your mother or father to switch off their Hindi music and puts an English station on. Sometimes Abhay comes home from work at around half past three in the afternoon so tired that he just wants to sleep and switches off the radio. With Chameli and Juhi, you discover new music, and enjoy the old stuff. There is a popular song of the time, "Ice Ice Baby," by Vanilla Ice. Juhi tries to memorize the lyrics. You enjoy watching the dancers and some steps in the music videos, and when you get home, you try doing them when no one is in the salon. Eventually you find out that you have a channel that puts music on at a certain time, and watch the dance steps carefully as you enjoy listening to the music. You practise them, until Shalini sees you doing some. She knows a few steps and teaches you some, while you teach her what you know.

One summer's night during school holidays Juhi, Chameli, Shalini and you stand outside Chameli and Juhi's driveway talking. Vivek is with a group, around fourteen of them are together. They call you all. They decide to play three tins and gather more people. In the end, you are something like twenty-five in total. You are often the usual ones who hang out on the street. The daughter of the Muslim man who Abhay made angry one Diwali never joins the rest of the kids, and hardly ever comes out of her house. Luckily, most kids on the street don't have big age differences from one another. Three tins is an interesting version of the game "Hide and Seek." Finding three tins on the street is easy. It's normal to find tins of coca cola, fanta, sprite etc. Someone piles up the three tins, and then fairly choose the seeker. You pray it isn't going to be you. When you are a seeker in Three Tins you don't have fun and it's possible that you can be the seeker forever. Luckily, neither of you four end up being the seeker. The game starts by someone kicking the three tins as far as they can. Then the seeker ends up running for the tins and quickly piles them up to how they were before. The seeker then has to start looking for those hiding away. The first one he catches is the one to start seeking next, however that person can be saved if a person comes out from his or her hiding place when the seeker is far away from the tins. He or she will run as fast as their legs can carry them and kick the tins as far as he or she can. The seeker has to run back and put the tins into place, those caught before hide away again and it continues until all twenty-five are caught. In this case it's impossible for the seeker to find all twenty-five of you, because you have the whole street to hide in. If you want to cut the seeker some slack and think it's enough, you all just opt for not saving anyone and stay in your hiding place, or after a certain time you all decide to make the first person caught the seeker so that everyone can enjoy themselves too.

When the game starts, you want to find a really good hiding place, and decide to go and hide in a tree behind a wall. You head for the tree which belongs to your opposite neighbour, climb the wall, and sit on the first branch, you lift your legs onto the branch so that no one can see you. Suddenly, Pitu comes onto the branch where you're sitting on and tries getting on but falls off, you make him more space while he gives it another go. You hope he'd hurry for once, before he ends up getting you both caught. This time he makes it. You are worried that the branch is going break, but it's too late to change hiding places. You both stick on until the seeker finds someone else before you. After twenty minutes, you both decide to get out of the tree to see what's happening; you can't hear or see anything from where you both are. You both see at least ten people around the seeker and so you both decide to head in his direction. It's now late to continue playing so you all decide to head home.

Your opposite neighbour has family ties with Mitali's family. Sometimes you ask your opposite neighbour how Mitali's doing or to send her your regards. One weekend while hanging around in your outside yard, you see Mitali; she comes to visit your neighbour and sees you outside. She comes to talk to you. So much time has passed and she still remembers you. She's very happy to see you and tells you she now works at Delta Spar part-time.

For some time now, you hear some people on the street calling Shalini "Olive." It often makes her angry. You too don't like her being called an ugly character in an animated cartoon "Popeye the sailor man." When you stand up for her she tells you off. Now you're going to standard six in high school, and are nervous of losing your friends; not being in the same class as them means that you have to make new friends. Your sister makes you scared and says that you might get initiated. She says she remembered that last year some people put a short standard six-year-old boy in the school dustbin on his first day of school, they also made another boy sweep a part of the assembly area and surrounded one boy creating a circle around him and making him dance inside. You hope that they don't end up teasing you the way they tease Shalini.

Now in the Nineties

You have short, pitch-black hair almost like a boy.
Spiked, like a Chinese. Your skin is white as in powder
white. You have thick eyebrows too. You look damn
cool. You have a short sleeve shirt on. It's loose and
you have good, toned muscles on your upper arms,
which hide under your sleeves. You have tight navy
blue stretch pants on. You are sitting on the desk with
your shoes on the chair. You are watching a boy and a
girl. They both bully you. The guy is popular in class,
and is dancing with the girl inside a circle. Your
classmates are surrounding them and clapping at the
way they dance. The guy who bullies you has a big
head, pitch-black hair in a style of a mushroom. He has
thick eyebrows, way thicker than yours. It actually
looks like a jungle, yuck! You can't imagine what lives
in there. He looks a little like the girl Pitu likes. He
looks almost exactly like her. You don't think he
dances so well. None of their moves are complicated or
interesting. A friend of his sees you sitting on the table
watching the show. She comes to you, pulls you off the
table, and drags your tiny body to the group saying,
"Look what I've found, she was sitting on the table
watching you!" Everyone around the circle pushes you
and dumps you in the centre and the bossy popular girl
who was making the moves in the centre exclaims,
"Surely you don't even know how to dance. You know
shit!" You have a pair of sunglasses in your shirt pocket
you pull them out cooly and put them on. The girl that
dragged you into the centre is in your space and looks
at you from bottom up. You walk towards her like
you're going to hit her, she steps back with
intimidation. You do the same to the guy who bullies

you and the girl standing with him. You drop down cooly, but have your eyes fixed on them, fold your pants up and stop just above your ankles. Now everyone can see your white socks. You undo a few buttons from the bottom of your shirt, until you get to your belly button. You knot your shirt showing off your waist. You pull out your winter leather gloves and put them on. You step back and move forward a little than lift your one leg up high gracefully, while your hands cross in front of you as you gracefully take them out, your hand stops just in front of the faces you want to hit while your leg goes back into position. You step and move and step and move and kick and step and move, you move forward go back and spin until one hand hits the ground. While doing that you pull out one of your legs, now you ready to breakdance.

You are doing all sorts of crazy moves and then stop your quick show when the teacher walks in. You all run and sit at your desks. You quickly take out a book and open it. The teacher leaves again, as you sit there reading. The girl that danced in the circle suddenly puts her hands around your body over your hands, trying to keep you stiff from moving your hands. You try to get free and see the guy who bullies you heading straight for you. He looks like he is ready to hit you. You push back your head and bang the head of the girl who tries holding you stiff. She lets go of you while she tries to recover. The girl that dragged you into the circle takes the place of the girl who's still recovering after the knock you've given her. She tries to keep you stiff. Again, you push your head backwards and hit her head. She falls to the ground. The guy coming for you puts one hand on one side of the table and the other on the other end of the table. He is pushing the table against you so that you can't get out. He is trying to make your chair fall back. You try to get out but you can't, you take your hands out straight and move them out in opposite directions to push his two hands off the table. His face hits the table, you go down into your chair, the guy's legs are wide open, and your legs are just below his groin, you kick him between his legs and he falls to the ground.

"Seash waaaaaaake uuuuuuuup! Seash wwwwwwwwwwwwwwwwwake up!" you wake up and find your head dangling from side to side. Shalini is trying to wake you up for school. While your head dangles left to right you say in your mind "Wwwwwwwwwwwwwhy, oh! Why is it just a dream, if only I can dance that well or do those karate moves for real." Last night you saw Kickbocker and some music videos of Michael Jackson.

It is the first day of high school. It's mid January, in the year 1992. You are now in standard six. You take a bath and you're now dressed for school. Your uniform is a white shirt, tucked into navy blue pants. Fortunately, they aren't like the ones you dreamt of before waking up. These are a little baggy and much more comfortable. You're sitting at the table trying to drink your tea, but you are very nervous, and don't know what to expect today. You know that today you will be divided into classes. You are scared to split up from your friends. Going early to school today is frightening. Luckily, you have Shalini with you.

Shalini is wearing her school skirt. You don't want to

108

look like her because you don't want people to tease you. Shalini's skirt is long and goes over her knees. She has socks that go just up to her ankles. Her legs are straight and have no shape since her long skirt is covering them. Her legs look like sticks. You prefer wearing pants because you have legs just like hers.

You walk into the school gates, and see an open area. As you enter the area, someone screams, "Look! Olive and Olive Junior! Haahaahaa." Shalini looks bothered but tries to ignore it. You think, "Just great! I hope I don't get called more names today, I might have to live with it for eternity." You look around and say to yourself, "Luckily, there aren't many people in this area that heard what he said." Your biggest fear is that if people start calling you names, your friends won't hang around with you anymore. You are hanging around with Shalini and her friends in the meanwhile and start to look for the faces you know. More so, you are looking out for your friends. You finally see them and leave Shalini's side to stand with them.

You are all standing in the same row and now they are going to put you in different classes. You don't know exactly how you are all going to be divided. A friend who you hung around with during break times in standard five starts skipping lines so that she can be with another friend. You too want to be with them, but you are too afraid of doing the same thing she's doing. You stay where you are and end up in a class with the girl Pitu liked in standard five. You wonder to yourself looking at the girl Pitu liked, "Just great! I had a dream of someone like you and now I'm here in the same class as you." The girl Pitu liked is called Asika. She was in your class in Standard Five. She had her own group of friends then, where she usually was the boss and had things her own way. Now she is alone here and you aren't very close to her. You look around your class and recognize some faces, but most of these people weren't in your class last year. The scary part now for you is, "break time." The question is, "Where are my friends from last year? Which class are they in? Are we all completely separated now? Will they come and look for me during lunch break? Does this mean we're not friends anymore? Does this mean that they have new friends now?" You have thousands of questions going through your mind right now. You make friends with a girl who was in another primary school last year. Asika also decides to make friends with her. Finally it's break time. You all seem lost. You, the girl you made friends with, and Asika decide to stick together even though no one says anything. You are very shy, and afraid of people teasing you. The three of you take a walk together and try not to wander off too much. You try finding your friends and think eventually they will come and find you. With them, you are so much more confident and now without them you are lost. Two days, three days, the fourth day goes by, and you now see it clearly that they aren't coming to look for you.

Dividing you all into classes separates your whole group from last year. "Perhaps each one made their own friends or maybe they don't want me with them," you wonder. You decide to stick with the friends you have now. Chameli has her group. She meets Hasini during break time. Mathematics is hard, and the teacher looks strict. You visit Chameli and Juhi somedays after school. During the weekends, you don't have anyone to hang around with. Asika is bossy and nasty. She always talks badly about others, laughs at them and has a big mouth. The other girl who you both made friends with the first day is bad but not as much as Asika. You know that one day Asika's mouth is going to get her into trouble. Right now for you it seems better to have bad friends than no friends at all. You just make sure about not getting into trouble with people.

You are getting bored at home. Abhay looks like he's tired of his current job; going everyday during summer and winter from four in the morning to four in the afternoon. He feels very cold in the winter where he works and there is no heating. He wears gloves and some jackets, but still gets sick. Right now, it is summer and Abhay hardly has a life and sleeps most of the time. He has sinus problems. You think a lot about Abhay, and about how long it took him to find a job. You feel sorry for him and know how hard it is for him to find a job. Everyone used to tell Abhay that he didn't have experience and for that reason, they aren't going to hire him. You start to think of looking for a part-time job, but don't know where to start. You think that right now you can do with extra money; do something useful with your life and time, but most of all you want to start young so that when you look for a job when you're older people don't end up telling you what they keep telling Abhay, "You don't have enough experience!"

A step to your future

You ask your opposite neighbour if she knows anyone
who can give you a part-time job. Things work out and
before you know it, you start working at Delta Spar. A
van comes to pick you up for work. It is your first day
in Delta Spar, you see Mitali's mum and ask her what
you have to do. She tells you where to stand. You work
in the same part as Mitali and also meet another girl
called Virsha, who is twelve years old. Virsha doesn't
know Mitali so well. Virsha herself is new and has only
been here for a few weeks now. She has black hair, a
bob haircut, medium built and is a very loud and happy
person. She often puts a black dot on her forehead. In
Gujarati, you call it "Chandlo" and in Hindi, they call it
"Bindi." Usually young women can wear any colour
Chandlo, and the black Chandlo means that you are
single. A married woman wears a red Chandlo. Bindi
also has something to do with the Chakras. Some Asian
cultures believe that there are energy centres in the
human body. This energy centre is called Chakra.

Every Saturday and Sunday morning, a van comes to
pick you up for work. Sometimes you even go to work
on Fridays after school, when they're understaffed.
Delta Spar is in a poor mixed race community not far
from where you live. When you see these people, how
poor they are and their situations, it saddens you. Some
children make you feel superior, and shockingly people
your age too. You get used to this because it's like this
in general while working here. You wonder why there
aren't any coloured, white, or black people where you
live. The only white person you've met and spoken to
for a bit so far was your dad's boss. When you were

young your father sometimes took you to where he worked, sometimes he would take Vivek there too. Your father is a salesman. He works in a big shop, which is divided into snacks, groceries, furniture, and DIY tools. One person owns the whole place where your father works. He helps people with what they are looking for, certain DIY tools, luggage bags and other things. He also works behind the till. Mainly black people who work in the mines nearby come there to shop. Your father knows a few words in the African language and says he knows Swahili well. He often mentions that he was in Kenya, Mombasa. He spoke about how big the fruits in Kenya were. In Kenya, people speak Swahili. Swahili is a Bantu language and there are hundreds of dialects spoken in central, east and southern Africa. Bantu is a tribal group that extends over a large part of Africa. Swahili is the official language of some African countries. It has some Arabic, Portuguese, German, English, Persian and French words. There are four racial groups at this moment in South Africa and they are whites, blacks, the mixed race group, known as coloureds, and lastly Indians.

Somedays are really hard at Delta Spar. Mitali's mother is nice but there is another woman who is the wife of the real owner of Delta Spar. She's strict and if Mitali's mum isn't giving you orders than this woman is busy giving you orders. This woman wears a sari, she's strict, and young. She plaits her hair and then makes a bun out of it. Her hair always looks shiny. You sometimes look at her and wonder on the days she's nice with you, "How beautiful she must look if she lets her hair loose." On the days she makes you mad you

113

say to yourself while looking at her raving on, "You need to let your hair down man!" One day you get a strict order by Mitali's mother and just as you are about to do it, the strict woman comes. She says, "Go and get twelve big white oil drums from the supermarket and put them outside. We are going to sell them." Man you hate this about this job. You stress and try to finish off what Mitali's mother gave you but it's taking too long. You say to yourself, "I'll come back and do it." You run over to the supermarket, get the big drums, and put them outside the shop. You get about ten, but think, "Ok if they get sold quickly then I'll just go for more." You come back and Mitali's mum says, "Why isn't this done?" Your fear usually stops you from explaining. She says, "Just finish it!" While you finish it, the strict woman comes and says, "Why are there ten drums outside, I told you to put twelve, go and get the other two and put them there!" You don't know how to explain because you're scared. You go and put the other two drums and find that the strict woman made a sign saying, "Twelve drums for sale." Now you see why she's mad. The sign says twelve and there's only ten. This happens a lot and it stresses you out.

You get your pay and buy something you always had your eye on while working at Delta Spar. You buy a nice diary with a lock. You decide that it could be a diary where your friends can write something in, anything, so that in the future you can read it and remember them. It doesn't matter to you if they are really good friends or friends with whom you hang around with. One day you go to Juhi and Chameli's house. You find Chameli and Hasini there. You hang around with them for a bit and ask them if they would

like to write something in your diary. They say, "Ok."
You go home and read it. It's really nice. You decide to
take the diary to school. It's break time and you pull out
your diary. You ask Asika and the other girl, "Do you
want to write something inside? It's for the future, so
that I can remember my friends." Asika opens the diary
and asks, "What should I write?" She opens the first
page and wants to read what Chameli and Hasini wrote,
so you shout, "No you can't read what Chameli and
Hasini wrote, it's personal!" You know that Asika can
cause trouble for nothing. Chameli and Hasini could be
upset if they find out that you showed others what they
wrote when it was only for your eyes. Knowing Asika,
she'll make fun of what they wrote and make it obvious
to them. She is a real troublemaker. Sometimes people
from higher standards called Asika "Big Head." She
has a really big head. When you hear them teasing her
and see her face, then you think enthusiastically,
"Yeah! Take some of your own medicine."

When you see Hasini and Chameli during break times
you greet them. They now hang around with two other
girls who you don't know. One day like many others
you greet them and Asika and the other girl laugh
sarcastically. As you leave, they keep looking back and
laughing. They always laugh at others so you just
ignore them. They start calling Hasini and Chameli
"Laurel and Hardy." "Laurel and Hardy" is a comedy
cartoon series. One character's name in the series is
"Stan Laurel." He's often called "Stanley" in the series.
Stanley is thin. The other character's name is "Oliver
Hardy." He's called "Hardy" in the series. Hardy is fat.
Chameli is tall and thin so she must be "Laurel" and
Hasini is short and fat so she must be "Hardy." Some

weeks pass and the teasing gets too much for you, so you can just imagine how frustrated Chameli and Hasini must be. You don't think it's funny anymore. You tell Shalini what's going on. She laughs when she hears what your friends call Chameli and Hasini. She says, "You don't have to worry, because it's not you teasing them, it's your friends. If something happens you're not involved." You agree, at the end it's not you causing trouble. One day Asika and the other girl have to meet the maths teacher in an area during breaktime. They are worried. Since you hang around with them, and are not use to being alone during break times, you decide to go too. You know it's best if you don't go with, but since you don't know who to hang around with break time you decide to go with them. You find Chameli and Hasini there too. Now you realize what this is all about. The teasing got so bad that it involves the maths teacher now. Hasini and Chameli complained to the maths teacher about Asika and the other girl. When Asika sees the teacher with Chameli and Hasini, she's scared. The mathematics teacher asks, "What's going on?" Chameli and Hasini points to Asika and her friend saying, "These two are calling us Laurel and Hardy." Asika and the other girl don't know what to say and try going round in circles, they can't find an excuse. You wonder, "Good this teaches you to stop looking for trouble now!" It looks like Asika doesn't have a way out, then suddenly Asika says, "It all started with the diary." You are in shock, and know this has nothing to do with you. The teacher asks, "What diary?" Asika points to you and say, "Her diary." You are saying in your mind, "wowowow, what does it have to do with that or me? I wasn't called here today. No way, she's looking for someone to blame." Everyone looks at you. The teacher asks, "What diary?" You explain but not very well, because you don't have confidence in yourself and are scared of the teacher. Asika says, "We wrote something in it, but she didn't let us read what they wrote. We thought it was because they wrote something bad about us." The maths teacher lifts her hand, and, "PAAA" before you even realise what happened your face hurts and turns to the other direction. She just slapped you in front of everyone. Everyone in this part of the school turns to look at you. "It is not even close to half year in my first year of high school, and now people will always look at me strange," you cringe with embarrassment. You say to yourself angrily, "Asika's name fits her." In Sanskrit Asika means "Daggar sharp." To you she's a backstabber. With that slap it's clear that the blame's on you, yet you didn't tease or look for problems with anyone. It's a messed up day, you just want to go home and cry. A teacher, an adult doesn't even know who deserves to be taught the rightful lesson. You tell Shalini what happened and she laughs about it. Lately Shalini laughs at almost everything bad that happens to you. You go to your room in tears, you look for the diary throwing around things which lay on top of it, and rip off the stained pages that caused today's events. You don't see the point of having this diary and throw it into a box under your bed, which is full of unused books.

Virsha, Mitali and you work together and have a lot of fun together. You are often serious when you work and sometimes playful but still do your work. Mitali and Virsha always put the music on almost full blast and are girls who don't fear too much. You don't think of doing what they do, because you are too scared. Mitali's mum is the supervisor, while Virsha's aunty owns the store. You become good friends with Virsha. Your boss's name is Tikku, but you all have to call him Tikku Bhai. He is the manager of Delta Spar. You are afraid of Tikku Bhai. He is almost bald and has just a few grey hairs left. He has a big belly and looks very strict. When he gets angry he looks like a pitbull, and you really don't want to be in his way. He doesn't smile and if he says hello it sounds like he's growling. Actually, for you his name matches his character. "Tikku" in Gujarati means "Strong," as in spicy hot enough to make you cry. Tikku is a Gujarati word. His strong voice and strict face can really make someone like you cry. Tikku Bhai knows your character well and uses his position to instill fear into you. You are a tiny girl for your age, tiny is fine but in most people's eyes, you're too skinny for your age. People often judge you by your size. You get nervous and scared easily, even when you do nothing. A stranger just has to give you bad looks or shout at you a little to drop your confidence. You get so scared that it even affects your voice and you end up like a little mouse answering with a little squeak when Tikku Bhai speaks to you. His voice is like thunder.

Now working very hard doesn't seem to count. You receive your salary every weekend and lately your salary isn't complete. At first, you think it's a mistake but when the same thing happens the week after you realize that "Tikku Bhai" is cutting your salary. You tell Virsha one day, and she says, "That's wrong, go and speak to him and find out what's going on." You know she's right and you decide to confront him.

You finally get the courage to confront him. The day comes, when you receive your salary. He calls people one by one using the loudspeaker. When he calls people he usually sounds strict, as if someone did something wrong, and one never knows if it's going to be for a good or bad reason. At the beginning you used to tremble but now you are used to pay day. His voice is deep and serious. "Saaaaeeesha come to the office!" You head up to his office. Today you just don't know how to pose the question, that you even consider making do with the salary he's giving you. Virsha keeps motivating you to speak to him. You come to the office and slowly close the door. You sit down in front of him. He hands you your envelope. You try to speak loud instead of squeaking like a mouse, you say "Sorry Tikku Bhai. I have a question?" He says nicely, "Yes." You say, "Why did I receive less money the last three weeks?" He is hesitating, it seems like he's looking for an answer. He says confidently, "Because you play around too much instead of working." He says it so seriously that your confidence drops. You say, "Ok," get up from the chair and leave. You know that you don't play around, so that is not a good answer. Virsha asks, "Did you ask him?" You say, "Yes." She says, "Soooooo tell me what he said?" You reply, "He said that he cut my salary because I play around too much instead of working." Virsha knows it's not true. It is now clear to you as to why Tikku Bhai cuts your wages instead of cutting Mitali's or Virsha's salary. You aren't related to the people who own Delta Spar but Virsha is and Mitali's mother is the supervisor who closely works with him. Virsha always teases Mitali's mum when you are both alone. When she sees Mitali's mother with Tikku Bhai she says, "Something is going on between those two." As weeks go by you feel embarrassed to get into the ugly Delta Spar van when it comes to pick you up. Vivek's friends are sometimes outside when the van comes to pick you up. It is so ugly inside, that you feel like you all are shoved together like a bunch of sheep. It takes time to kill the feeling of embarrassment, as you bravely convince yourself that it doesn't matter what people think, and besides you don't have many friends anyway. You are doing something useful with your time, earning money and being at Delta Spar at least keeps you busy rather than being bored at home.

At school, you stop hanging around with Asika and the other girl after what happened. You think having no friends is better. You don't want anymore trouble. At school, you are hanging around by yourself, and it really sucks. You don't have much to talk about or do. People give you strange looks and you look around you and say, "I mean everyone has friends. Why is it so difficult for me?"

You still have the same style of writing compositions, like the ones you wrote in primary school. The topics are difficult now; they're not like the topics in primary school. Now you don't have much of an imagination. You're having problems but you don't think it's big. You write what comes into your mind and never think about it. Sometimes you don't have much knowledge of the subject. Your teacher is nice, and you all call her "Mrs Spears." One day you write a composition in the class about a subject given. You look around you and everyone is writing a lot. Only you are at the second paragraph and nothing is coming to your mind. You have to hand it in that same day before the class is over. You look at your English teacher, "She's a nice teacher," you wonder. You write, "Madam Spears is one of the best English teacher's I know." It seems related to the topic and you put it in because it's something positive. Things are not flowing to your mind, which means it's time to think. You continue with the composition and try to think of ideas that correspond to the subject. The next day you receive your composition mark. It's a four out of ten. Your marks in composition usually sit at around six out of ten.

A few days pass, until one day while finishing some work given to you all in your English class the teacher calls out your name very loudly, breaking the silence in the class. She says with a serious tone, "Saesha! Stand up!" You stand up slowly, and your confidence drops when the whole class turns their heads in your direction. Mrs Spears tells you seriously, "Look at your skirt!" You look down at your skirt. "It's not even cleaned properly, and your shoes are so dirty." You look at your shoes, they aren't dirty, you can't believe this is even happening at this age. She says, "Look up!" You don't want to be here. Your core is saddened that someone has taken the opportunity to do this in front of the class. Your heart is hurt, you're holding in the tears, and are so embarrassed yet try to look at her, but your hair is in front of your left eye. You have to look at her so you take your left hand and push your hair behind your ears slowly. She says, "And your hair, you're always pushing it back with your hands." As far as you know your skirt is clean, after primary school you always pay attention. She says, "You should take pride in your dressing, and your work! Now you can sit down!" You sit down slowly, everyone is looking at you and you wonder sarcastically to yourself, "Now you have a really nice day Saesha!" During the day, you wonder to yourself if you really look that bad. You look at some class mates, and there are some people who are dressed worse than you. It's break time, you don't want to go anywhere. You just want to sit in the class. You tell Shalini what happened after class and take a look at your skirt and think, "Mum washes by hand and it's not so dirty."

The next day, Asika sees you in the morning. She's with the other girl. You wonder to yourself, "She must enjoy what she saw yesterday!" Asika comes to you and tells you, "You know my mother said that what the teacher did yesterday was wrong. She can't do that in front of everyone in the class." You say softly, "Yeah, whatever!" You wonder to yourself while looking at Asika, "Why do you care all of the sudden?" and turn and walk into class. You wonder, " What's the point if the teacher was wrong, if you even have a mother to begin with. She doesn't help you, and if she finds this out, she'll do nothing about it. She won't even know what to do." Ever since no matter how hard you try and no matter whose help you get, your compositions are never good enough. Shalini has been taking you to her friend to get help in your compositions. You keep trying and keep trying, as English is the main subject. Failing english means you have to repeat the whole year. You actually believe that it doesn't matter if you study or not, this teacher is going to fail you anyway. You are afraid that you will have to repeat the whole standard again until one day your composition mark changes for the better.

One day as you hang around by yourself, Chameli and Hasini call you, and you start to hang around with them during breaks. It's already a few weeks now that you're hanging out with Chameli and her friends. During break time one day Chameli and her friends crack a joke, it is so good that you laugh into tears. You normally return a few minutes earlier to class from break time and always find Pravashni and Farzana together. Pravashni's hair is curly and in layers. It goes right down to the middle of her back. Her hair is shiny and the curls are between medium and small. She is plumpy but has a very radiant character. Her smile goes right across her face. Her lips are full and she looks like the shining sun every time she smiles. Pravashni smiles a lot. She is a very confident person, very open and loud. Her eyes are big. When she sees you, she has a big warm smile. Farzana is a girl who stays in an adoption house. She's Pravashni's best friend at school. She usually wears a Hijab and has her hair plaited. It is normal to see almost all Muslim girls wear a Hijab during Ramadan. Some even wear the Hijab when it isn't Ramadan. A Hijab is like a scarf that many Muslim women and young girls use to cover their head. Ramadan is in a month during the Islamic year. During this month Muslims have to fast, ie; they can't drink, eat, have sex, smoke during daylight. The fast starts early morning and is broken after sunset. Fazana and Pravashni are friendly and often talk to you while you wait for break time to be over.

One Friday you plan to visit Juhi and Chameli. You come out of your house and walk to the front gate. You stop in your tracks because you're hearing some arguments coming from their house. You think it's not a good time to visit them. You go back to your front door, but on the way to the door, you hear your name in the argument. You can hear vaguely but when Chameli raises her voice you hear her clearly and realize what it's about. "She's embarrassing to hang around with!" Juhi says, "Be friends with her! So what if others think that!" It sounds like Chameli doesn't want to hang around with you break times. You think of going to hang out with them. You don't listen to the whole argument and don't know where things stand. You think that if they make it clear to you and say that you can't hang around with them than you'll just accept it.

Friendship

Virsha and you become good friends and meet up on a regular basis. Virsha lives in town and you live a little bit far from her. It takes you thirty minutes to walk to her house and five minutes by car. You often walk to her house. You hang out together after work, at weekends, on public holidays, and school holidays and learn to play pool. Some Fridays you are both called in for work if Delta Spar is understaffed while on some Fridays you are free. If you both aren't together at work, than you both are busy hanging out together. Fridays after school, you both have a place where you usually hang out. You stay over at her house during weekends a lot and she comes to stay over at yours one day. Virsha and you are in different schools, and you wish that Virsha could come to your school. She'll turn thirteen this year. With all the friend problems you're having at school you realise what a real friend should be like. Virsha becomes your best friend. You swear to yourself that you will look after this friendship since she's the only friend who accepts you for you.

Virsha's sister, Shariksha is a little older than you and Virsha. She is beautiful, has long thick hair, and she looks older than she really is. She has full lips, and puts light pink lipstick on. She isn't like you or Virsha. You both wear pants most of the time. Virsha doesn't like dresses and neither do you but at least she wears shorts but you are too shy to wear them. You are not into boys, you like other things more than boys, and that's dancing. Virsha doesn't have a boyfriend and you both are very much alike. Shariksha dresses like a woman and seems popular with people especially guys, and hanging out with her is pretty cool. She is around sixteen years old but hangs around with guys who are around twenty five years of age. She takes you and Virsha to nightclubs, restaurants and bars to make your weekends more interesting. Shariksha has men chasing after her all the time. Somedays it's extremely hot to walk to Virsha's house, the trees hardly give shade along the way, and besides there aren't enough trees. You hardly see Juhi and Chameli, and visit them very little now. Fridays after school you first go to Virsha's house. Virsha and Shariksha are always finishing the chores their mum gave them when you arrive. Virsha has to vaccuum the house while Shariksha does hers. When Virsha's mum comes home she asks them, "Did you do the things I told you both to do?" Virsha sometimes says yes even if she didn't do it.

One evening Virsha's mum surprises you all, she comes in after arriving from work and asks the usual question, "Did you both do the cleaning?" It's as if they're in the choir when they say, "Yes mum we did it." Virsha's mum pushes the sofa a bit and finds a little white ball. She says to Virsha, " Aha! You didn't do the vacuuming." Virsha laughs and says, "You set up a trap for me to see if I clean properly." You all laughed because she set up a trap to find out if Virsha vacuums the carpet. Virsha and Shariksha enjoy their mums company. She's fun, and only strict on very few occasions.

One day Shalini gets a call. The person says, "Virsha just met up in an accident." When you find out you go straight to her house. You take a walk but try to run more than walk. It's hot, you worry about Virsha and finally manage to get to her house. You get to the door and ring the bell. Virsha opens the door. You scream, "You're ok, thank god!" She looks at you as if you're mad and say, "What are you talking about?" You say, "Someone called my house and said that you were in an accident." She and Shariksha laughed. You say, "Someone must have played a prank on me, well at least you weren't in an accident." You take a walk back home, since it's not too late. It's dark outside but there are still people on the street.

Virsha and Shariksha's mum is in her second marriage, being constantly around them you get to know their parents. Whenever you stay over at their home, Prenesan Virsha's stepfather shows you exercises to strengthen weak points in your body for karate. He is tall and big built. You see how he does it and you copy him but then he takes your ankles, shows you properly how to strengthen it, and does the same to your wrists. You want to learn karate and Prenesan always boasts that he knows and practices marshal arts for years. You have great interest in learning everything he teaches you. You are in fact surprised that they treat you so well.

The family is a normal family and you like it there quite a lot. Sometimes Virsha would ask you to have dinner with them and then ask Prenesan if he can drop you home. Sometimes Virsha comes to drop you off and at times not. The times that Virsha doesn't accompany you, you feel uncomfortable sitting on the front seat next to Virsha's stepfather. Some months go by and you start to feel a strange activity happening inside your body. It isn't a nice feeling but you can't understand it

127

and don't know what the hell it is. You don't know how to stop it, and think that if you tell anyone this than they will probably say, "You are strange." This might alienate people. You say to yourself, "It's probably just me; I seem to be the strange one most of the time." You ignore it and find that this activity happening inside you occurs mainly when you're around Virsha's stepfather.

You and Virsha are growing up together. You are thirteen, and hardly have any hair on your legs, yet Virsha thinks it's time for you to shave your legs. At first, you don't want to, but then you think that you are going to do it at some stage and than all your life anyway. You consider which way is the best for you; waxing or shaving. Shariksha waxes her legs and you don't want to go through pain. Virsha says,"Trust me! it's better to shave." You buy the aloe vera razor from work, which is popular right now. It isn't a normal throw away razor and apparently it leaves your legs silky smooth. The first time you shave your legs is at Virsha's house. It feels strange doing it. After doing it, and coming out of the shower, Virsha screams with so much excitement that it catches Prenesan's attention. This makes you shy and red. You don't feel comfortable talking about girls' things in front of him, and wish for Virsha to shut her big mouth.

As weeks go by the activity in your body becomes stronger, so strong that being around Prenesan makes you uncomfortable. You think you are not a normal child. You think perhaps everyone has these feelings and that it probably has something to do with growing up. You also think that probably everyone gets this feeling and talking about it can end up creating problems, but this problem won't be like the other problems you have, this problem can be bigger. You might even lose your friendship with this family and especially Virsha. You think and ask yourself, "What if I am not a normal child? What if I talk to someone and they start teasing me?" You decide to keep all this to yourself, and say, "It will pass by like everything else I have been through."

You hardly hang around at home during weekends. When you can see Virsha, you go without thinking. One evening, you come home early at night. Today you are home at around ten O'clock at night. Your mum and dad are watching television when you open the gate. It is a hot night so your family leaves the door open. As you come in Abhay comes into the salon saying to your parents, "You two are sitting here while Saesha goes out. You two don't even know where she goes, she's only thirteen." You know your brother is right. Sometimes you leave and do it more because you think that they just don't care about you. They never ask where you are going or what you'll be doing. Sometimes you leave and they don't even know when you left and you often ask yourself if they even care. You even tell them that you have been to a club at thirteen years of age and your father just keeps watching the television as if he heard nothing. Days after your mum asks innocently, "What do people do in a club?" She'd hear Abhay saying that word alot. You say, "We dance that's all. Others drink alcohol but we just dance." Abhay doesn't hang around with the guy he was best friends with anymore. One day he just stops coming to your house and you wonder what happened

129

between them.

One evening, Virsha calls you. She says, "Seasha I met up in an accident." You think it's a joke and say, "Come on I heard this one before." She says, "No I mean it, it really did happen!" You worry and ask, "Where are you calling from? Are you safe? How did it happen?" She says, "Don't worry I'm ok. I was crossing the street and I didn't see the car, it hit me and I fell to the ground. It was going slow and stopped after I fell to the ground. My shoe fell off, and the driver came out to see if I was ok." It's too late in the evening to take a walk to Virsha's house. When you hang up you tell Shalini what happened with Virsha and she laughs. She says, "Oh! my god! Now she really did meet up in an accident."

One day just like many other normal weekends at Virsha's house, you get up and hear her family in the salon, you wake up late today and decide to join them in the salon. You find them talking and joking around with each other as usual. Virsha, Shariksha and their mum get up and start walking to the room, they are excited to see something in the room. You don't join them since you understand that some things are for family and not friends, and besides you just sat down with them and think it will look odd if you suddenly get up to join them since you don't want to be left alone with Prenesan. You also don't want Prenesan to pick up your strange reactions. You don't want to be alone with Virsha's stepfather. Now you both are alone but you know it isn't going to be for long. Virsha, Shariksha and their mum will return at any moment now. Your back is slightly turned and you are partially facing

Prenesan. Prenesan starts to talk to you. He says, "I want to teach you some things, and prepare you for when you get a boyfriend, you should get used to people touching you on certain parts of you body, like here...", as he says that, he touches your neck, then touches your back running his fingers up and down you spine. He goes further down and you hope he isn't going to touch your bottom. You want it to stop. This feels like torture, and you pray for Virsha to come back. He is saying the body parts as he touches them. He than touches your bottom and says, "Here too." You feel alone, your mind is thinking rapidly, "It's not normal for Virsha to be away this long. What if I run to the door? What if he planned this a long time ago? Did they plan it together? No way Virsha won't do something like that, I mean she's my best friend. What if the door is locked? I'm still in pyjamas. Were do I go. What if I never leave this place, what if I die here?" You are now terribly afraid. You decide to pull this through until you safe at home. You still don't have it all figured out. The activity in your body is changing rapidly and causing reactions, You now feel sick but don't want to show it. You pretend as if you're normal. You start to convince yourself that what he's saying is making sense and then he asks you, "Don't you think you should get used to man touching you?" You think, "Saesha, just how will you get a boyfriend, if you don't let him touch you? What he is saying is right, I mean all the girls who have boyfriends allow their boyfriends to touch them." Your voice changes into an uncomfortable squeak and you think as much as you hate this you have to do it for your own good. You say unsurely, "Ok."

You take a deep breath when you hear Virsha's mother,

Shariksha and Virsha returning to the salon, Virsha's stepfather slides his hand back up, his hands are still on your back near to the shoulders and he acts as if everything is normal. You don't know how many minutes have passed but it felt like an hour when it really was way less. You look down and the activity in your body is making you sick even with his hand being on your back. Someone suggests, "It's time to make the bed!" Prenesan says, "Saesha and I will make the bed!" "It isn't over for me," you are screaming inside. At that moment you are wishing for your friends to save you but they are innocent and don't know what's happening. They say, "Yes, you guys go and make the bed!" You enter the room, he shuts the door and you are now afraid. You start to make the bed and just when you think he isn't going to do anything, he comes and stands in front of you. He puts his hand out straight, as one would do when they're about to cut through a ton of bricks in karate. He positions it between your legs and moves it upwards until it hits your vagina. It is as if he is doing karate, striking a layer of bricks, having their hand stiff and straight, moving downwards to break right through it, only here his hands are moving upwards. His hand hits your vagina and even if it didn't hurt, something inside you breaks. The activity in your body becomes too much too handle. He says, "You'll have to get used to this." You are still, you can't move, and don't know what just happened inside you. He puts his mouth onto yours. You are stiff yet he's holding you stiff and whirls his tongue about in yours. He takes it out, and you want to vomit. You can feel his slime in your mouth mixing with your saliva. You try to hold what's in your mouth there. It feels like something so disgusting that you don't even want to swallow it. If you swallow, than you are contagious or something. Your body has the urge to vomit badly. You stick it until the bed's made. You are stiff, the activity that just happened in your body makes you feel this way. You're still in shock and try to walk out of the room normally, but feel very sick. This moment feels worse than the last. It feels like a day has gone since you've seen Virsha. You didn't think you'd make it out of the room alive. As you walk out of the room Virsha and Shariksha notice your face and Virsha asks, "Saesha are you ok?" Your face is white! Completely white!" You feel sick and utter holding the slime in your mouth, "I feel like vomiting," and before anyone can say anything you run straight for the bathroom. Virsha and Shariksha follow you quickly. You close the door behind you and spit in the sink. Virsha wants to come in and you let her in, you can't vomit even if you try, you have an empty stomach but nothing comes out. You don't see Virsha's stepfather there. You say repeatedly to yourself in your mind, "I need to go home now. I need to go home now. I need to get out of here now. I can't do it anyhow, or I might just never get out of here." Virsha doesn't understand what is happening. You feel better after spitting out what was in your mouth. You decide to act normal until you shower and dress. Once that is done, you are going to make sure the door is open before you tell Shariksha and Virsha about what happened. You decide to shower first. You are feeling dirty that you don't even want to touch yourself. It's like your body is stained. This dirty feeling isn't coming off and when you come out you find out that Virsha's stepfather is gone out. You tell Shariksha and Virsha in the bathroom what happened and decide to go home. You tell Virsha that you can meet them somewhere in town this way you all can still hang out together.

Prenesan made plans some time ago to go to Pietermaritzburg tomorrow. You were excited when he suggested you come with them but now you're definitely not going to go. You know this is the last day that you step into this house. You take a walk home. Now it's making sense. You go back to past memories, when he showed you things for karate, the way he tickled you, it was so that he could touch you. He often called you his girlfriend jokingly in front of his wife and kids. It all led to this. You blame yourself for what happened, "I'm so stupid, and why didn't I figure it out?" You keep calling yourself stupid. You remember watching once something about this. You remember a psychologist saying to a child, "It is never your fault." You try to remember what else you saw in the programme. You say to yourself, "aaaaa aaaaaaa I'm not blaming myself for this, I am just thirteen. If only mum made me smarter in these things." You remember what Virsha said when you told her, "Saesha you've just been molested by my stepfather!" You wonder "I don't even know what molested meant up to now, even my twelve year old friend knows what it is. What a way to find out, come on! There's even a word for what I've been through, How come I don't know something like this exists and surely my own family don't even know this word?"

You keep thinking on your way home, "I have to tell my family what happened." You start thinking more, and tell yourself. "I can't tell my family this. I don't want to tell them what happened. Virsha's stepfather will go to court for this. This can break their family up.

This can become so big that cousins, uncles and aunties will find out about it. Just imagine your mother's side of the family. They'll invent their own things from hearing the news from others. You are going to shame your whole family for this." Your mind is working fast and you think about your own family. Now you come to your senses. You wonder, "If at home there isn't any communication how are my parents going to face this. My family doesn't have the time and money to take this to court. What am I talking about? My father won't even go that far to handle this! My father will find an easy solution to this. He will tell me to forget this, and mummy is going to blame me for what happened. I can't communicate this to them it's difficult, it's an embarrassing issue. Come on! Just imagine how my brothers and sister will look at me. They will tease me for the rest of my life. Just imagine how dirty I will feel if I already feel dirty now." You keep wondering, "Just imagine what's worse, the fact that they will make me feel dirty all my life and that I will never forget this ordeal. That everyone will think of me as some slut. I still have to live with myself besides now I can forget about it. I'm sure things will get back to normal now. At least this is over." You make the decision, "This stays with me for the rest of my life I will just learn to live with it."

You arrive home and look for some privacy. You see your mum in the kitchen and she sees you. Often you never said hello or bye when you leave. Showing feelings of love and politeness in your house isn't normal. Right now, you hate the whole world. You hope that there is no one in yours and Shalini's room. You get under the bed sheets and start crying. You cry and keep it silent. You're still feeling dirty, and impure. Crying silently isn't working it's getting worse and just than someone walks into the room. You stay still and don't move. You pretend that you are asleep. You realize it's your father, because his cupboard is in your room. You get angry and swear in your mind, "In this damn house I don't even get to have my privacy, this isn't a normal house, it's an underworld!" Your father leaves, and you continue crying, and fall off to sleep.

Later that night Virsha calls. The incident keeps playing back and forth in your mind and you don't know how to stop it. Virsha asks you to come with them tomorrow. You say, "Virsha I can't, please don't ask me this." You can't speak that much because the telephone is in the salon and your parents are watching television. They can hear everything you say. Virsha starts to beg and says, "It's just this time and no more." You are frustrated that your friend is asking this of you, and then she says, "Me, my mum and Shariksha will protect you. We just want to see what he does. Act like nothing happened." You say, "Ok," Now you're scared about tomorrow, and you can't stand another day in his presence, but see why it's important that your friends and their mother see it clearly. You decide to be brave and will try to pretend as if nothing happened so that he won't be suspicious. You hope that he isn't suspicious now, because tomorrow if he doesn't act normal it's possible that you might look like a liar. Your only fear is that he might touch you, and that you don't want to go through it again.

They come to pick you up next morning. You smile and pretend everything is normal, but inside you are dying

to kill him. He talks to you like nothing happened and
calls you his girlfriend again. You jump in the back seat
and sit next to Virsha. As he drives, he keeps looking at
you from the rear view mirror. He says, "I prepared the
back of my station wagon for my girlfriend and Virsha.
They can see the view from the back and can even sleep
there. It's soft like a bed." Saying that you are his
girlfriend is sick, but at least it's better than being
touched. During the whole trip, he calls you girlfriend.
Finally, you all arrive. You get off and follow. You try
and stick like glue to Virsha, Virsha's mother and
Shariksha are behind you. You all walk into some
shops. He tries to get near you. He is hovering over you
like a buzzard, keeping his eye on you, trying to get
closer, he gets closer, you are nervous, and just than
Virsha, Shariksha and their mum closes him off. It's a
torture for you; you depend on them completely to
protect you. You get through this for three hours. He
keeps trying to touch you again and again, but you are
always saved. You are relieved when you arrive home.
After that day, you never return to Virsha's house and
you meet them outside their residence. Virsha tells you
one day, "Before your incident took place, one of my
friend's said something about Prenasan trying in on
with her, but nothing concrete happened."

When you meet Virsha, she tells you what is happening
at home. She and Shariksha confront their stepfather
about what he did to you. Virsha says to you, "When
we confronted him about his actions, in the beginning,
he denied it and then after a while he admitted it and
told me and Shariksha that he did it because you are
Gujarati." It looks like Virsha bought his crap. You
almost buy that crap too and tell yourself, "It's not my

fault that I am Gujarati. I didn't do anything to anyone. What does it have to do with me being Gujarati? I can't believe that my friends accept his actions for an answer like that." You don't understand because in the end, you and Virsha's family are still Hindu even if they are Tamils. Hindu comes from the term Hinduism a religion. Tamils are a race and most of them follow Hinduism. You remain good friends with Virsha and Shariksha knowing that one day they'll see the truth and so you still hang out with them like before.

Abhay puts Shalini down; he often calls her this word, "Waste!" He repeats it too much to her. Your parents hear it and do nothing. Fine your mother doesn't do a thing but your father is the one who is the boss of this house apparently, and he doesn't step in to stop Abhay from calling Shalini "A waste." Shalini lets him do it. You stand up for her and Abhay ignores you. The respect for your mother is lost, no one listens to her, and you, Abhay and Vivek tell her what you like. Your father hears you all and never stands up for her. Your father treats your mother how he wants; he doesn't even speak to her politely. Shalini and your mum are like best friends.

One day Abhay demands you to serve him like a Hindu woman should. You think your father is going to stand up for you, but your father tells you, "You must learn how to cook." He sits down on the table and expects you to pour him a cup of "Cha." Luckily, you still don't know how to make "Cha." "Cha" means tea in Gujarati. At home, it's common to brew cha with spices like many people do in your culture. Your father makes you angry, he often asks you to pour him cha when Shalini or your mum isn't around. You do it, but you are not very happy about it. Abhay comes from work and sits down to watch TV in the salon. He orders you around as if you are his slave "Bring me a glass of water!" You answer back and say, "Bring it yourself!" Shalini and your mum do everything for them, they even make all of their beds.

The Power

You have big, baggy, blue jeans on. You wear baggy T-shirts.

I'm gonna blast your heart,
I'm gonna blast the heart of hearts...
da da dadada, datatat-ta dadada. (Moving left to right)
Cross step and jump (moving right to left) Cross step and jump. Now spin, aaaaaaaaaaaand Break it down!
Jump up (land with your legs apart), and finally the wipers (A step that seems like car wipers starting from two opposite directions moving inwards and outwards to bring your legs back together). You scream, *"I've got the power!"*

At school, you join a group "MDDActive." Here you do arts and entertainment work after school on certain days. It isn't the most professional school for arts right now. It is an activity that some public schools have for people who enjoy music, dance and acting.
"MDDActive" stands for "Music, Drama, and Dance."
At MDDActive you get to know Pravashni better, she is with you in the programme and you both seem to have a lot in common. The school gets transport for those who join MDDActive. You and Pravashni have to go to Johannesburg for MDDActive.

You now have a new sense of style and buy things with your own money. You don't want to show any skin. You close your body off completely. All anyone can see is your skinny arms and face. You hate boys, and having this kind of style is anti boy protection, it makes you feel safe. In fact it's a good disguise and you like hip-hop. You've gotten better. Shalini even gets into it with you and teaches you new steps. Since Abhay and your father work, the salon is all yours. Vivek is never at home after school. That leaves you, Shalini and your mum. You always shut the door in the salon so that the music you dance to doesn't interfere with your mum's Indian radio station. Now you can do all kinds of moves with all kinds of beats.

Virsha has a boyfriend now. His name is Maxwell. The song "Maxwell's Silver Hammer" by the Beatles always comes to your head when Virsha says his name. Maxwell is cool. He's Christian, dark in complexion, tall and thin. He has short hair, which stops right by his lower neck. He thinks you're cool too, and that's not normal for you, since everyone thinks you're weird. He gels his hair and often touches his hair to see if it is set straight. Virsha always tries changing his style to how she likes it. Maxwell walks like a cool hip-hopper.

One day Virsha, Maxwell and you decide to go to the ice rink in Johannesburg. You never took a taxi on your own or with anyone else before. From Virsha's house, it's easier to catch the taxi. The taxi is a minibus, which fits in fifteen people including the driver. In South Africa, taxi accidents are common. Most drivers are reckless. Those who don't have cars take taxis. Virsha's mum takes a taxi to work. Right now, there is just one place and one taxi company in your town. The taxis go directly to Johannesburg. There are no buses taking you to other parts of Johannesburg. If you want to go to another part of Johannesburg, you would first get into Johannesburg and take a bus from there to go to where you want to go. The bus service in your town is not reliable; you don't know where it goes half the time. Most people have cars or rely on taxis. Taxis are faster. You know it's impossible for you to learn how to get around in Johannesburg and in other parts of Johannesburg. The transport system is a handicap to people. Virsha only knows how to get to Johannesburg and to the main places; the ice rink and cinema. You three go together, and it's your first time in a taxi. You sit by the window in the second row. Luckily, there are three seats together, so you all sit together. Those who come last in groups sit in the free seats. It's squashed, and hot. It's like you all are being packed into a tin. You hardly have space. This minivan is just made to transport all you fish. As the driver leaves, people gather their money. A person in every row collects the money and passes it to the front. Before the driver leaves town, he goes slowly counting everything. Normally who ever is in the front seat makes it easy for the driver to count it all, and off you go. The taxi stops at the taxi rank in Johannesburg. You all get off. Virsha takes you and Maxwell to the ice rink. You both like ice-skating and there, they also play nice music. Maxwell can't skate to save his life. You all get bored after a while. Virsha saw you dance a couple of times at the place where you all hang out on Fridays. She says, "Saesha, why don't you dance up there, next to the DJ. The way you dance makes everyone stare, surely people will stop skating to watch you dance." You say, "No, you know I only dance a little with you but never in front of a lot of people." You are dying with the desire to dance because the music that's playing right now is making your blood, body, and bones move, it's as if you have something inside you dying to show itself. Music just does something to you. It's like magic, like your core is trying to expel your outer layers converting you into a super dancer. You want to do it, but you worry it could backfire. Virsha convinces you and so does Maxwell. You go up with Virsha and Maxwell to the DJ and ask the DJ, "Can I dance here?" The DJ nods his head to tell you yes. Virsha exclaims, "She's professional you'll see!" You wait for a new song. You are standing in a wide space where the DJ is doing his work. You, Virsha and Maxwell are on something like a stage and the ice rink is below you. Virsha and her boyfriend Maxwell say, "Go Saesha!" as soon as the song starts. You begin to flow with the music; your body has a ripple effect, and as the beat rises, the effects get bigger and bigger. Something like a rain drop falling into a puddle. You know the song, its Madonna's, "Vogue." You've danced to it before. You love this song, and when you get like this, you just can't stop. You shake your head left to right, as if it's displaced from your body, you smile and wonder to yourself how long it took you to learn that move. It's thanks to bollywood, where you got that move from. You take your legs apart, and do some hand movements and jumps synchronising your moves and when you come to...

Come on fold,
Let your body move to the music,
Hey hey hey
Come on fold...

You do a very quick step improvising "The running man" and incorporate other movements going with the beat, and Virsha shouts, "Saesha everyone is looking, carry on, go, go, carry on!" You stop to look at the ice rink, and find that people even stop skating to look at you, you get shy. People look amazed; you know you still don't have the guts to dance in front of this many people. "Seasha, come on, carry on!" screams Virsha. You say, "I ran out of steps!" On the way home, Virsha is like, "Did you see that Max? Did you see it? Man she turned heads." Virsha is over the moon.

On Fridays, you meet Virsha and the gang. You often all go to a place where they make "He-man." "He-man" is an animated series for kids. One small take away restaurant has "He-man" in their menu. It's a long roll full of french fries spiced with vinegar, salt, chilli powder, and tomato sauce. Inside they even stack up Palony. You have the option to have mustard and ketchup on top. You were born in the caste that doesn't eat meat, however once in primary school Asika gave you a sandwich. You were very hungry so you ate it knowing there was Palony inside. You liked it so much. Even though you liked it you swore you will never eat meat again.

Now with Virsha buying a He-man it is normal. You all share it because it's so big. You don't want to complain. When you receive your piece of the He-man, you take out the palony and offer it to Virsha but it's impossible to take out all of it. Virsha says, "Saesha just eat it, nothing's going to happen!" You enjoy the He-man and the palony, but you feel you have sinned. You go home and find your mum washing dishes and you ask, "Mum, why are we vegetarian?" She says, "Go and ask your father." You say, "Ok" and march over to where your father is sitting. He is in the salon. You ask your father, "Dad, why are we Vegetarian?" Your dad says, "Go and ask your mother." You say, "I just asked her and she told me to come and ask you." Your father sits still and watches the television. You wait for an answer stupidly, until you realise he is not going to give you one. You try to remember the Ramayana. A Hindu sage Valmiki wrote the Ramayana; a story of a Prince called Rama. It is written in Sanskrit at least over one thousand five hundred years ago. It is said to be an epic based on facts. There are two epics, these epics show the belief of reincarnation. You remember a part in the story. When Rama was living in the jungle, he clothed himself with animal skin. You say to yourself, "Rama is a god, now if he clothed himself with animal skin, than as a god he can't just waste its remains. Surely, he didn't hunt just for skin. AHA!" You come to the conclusion and say, "If my parents don't know, and if the story isn't making sense and eating meat is a sin than I don't believe everything about Hinduism." Slowly you eat meat more often with Virsha, until one day the take away restaurant runs out of He-man. Another girl goes to buy the He-man this time, and brings a roll with some meat and chips. You ask Virsha, "What meat is it?" She says with fear, "I don't know?" You both trust that it's not beef. Now you are worried sick that if you eat beef than that would be a sin. While eating it, you can't handle it. It's meat, its flesh, it's working on your mind and you are not used to this kind of meat. Virsha and you find out it's beef. She spits it out, and throws the rest of it away, you too do the same. You start to feel sick, and vomit it all out. Distastefully you say to Virsha, "I don't think I'm going to eat meat after this!" Virsha says, "It's not a sin if we didn't know." The cow is a symbol of life in Hinduism and often referred to as "Gau Mata" in India. "Gau" is cow and "Mata" is mother, just as a mother provides milk for her children cows produce milk for humanity.

One day as you, Pravashni and the others who joined MDDActive are in the minibus. You are all coming home from Johannesburg in the minibus. On the highway you see an accident on the opposite oncoming lane, it occupies almost the whole road. Your minibus stops inside the yellow lane. The driver jumps out quickly and runs across to the highway on the other side. You can all see the sight of the crash from the window. You all jump out and run to the highway across. The area where the accident took place is clear, and there is no traffic. It is a minibus taxi, just like the ones you and Virsha took when you went to Johannesburg. The seats are ripped out of the taxi while some are intact. There's blood and the sound of people crying. You go to some people lying on the floor. You find the ripped out seats on the floor and some with people still on them. You are a kid and most of these people from the crashed taxi are adults. You wonder, "What can I do?" You feel helpless. You jump back into your minibus with the group. You have the visual memory of the still bodies. As you are heading back home the whole group is silent.

Getting Active

"AAAAAAnd up and down, up and down, up and down, AAAAAAAAAAAAaaand hold! 1, 2, 3, 4, 5, 6, 7, 8, 9 and 10. Now relax." You can't keep up. "MAAAAAAAAAN why is Pravashni so good at everything?" you think to yourself. Your stamina is always low in the last fifteen minutes. It's three months gone and Pravashni can already do the splits, but you are not too far from her.

It's 1993. You and Pravashni join MDDActive this year too. You both are inseparable at MDDActive. You both love dancing. This year MDDActive takes place at a school in a coloured community, which you are familiar with. Delta Spar isn't far from the school. In MDDActive Pravashni and you meet two boys, both around 18 years of age and they dance hip-hop. Their names are Mark and Cris, and they show you how to do some crazy steps. With all these new steps, you are becoming such a great dancer and with MDDActive, you are slowly losing your shyness. Mark and Cris are cool people and talented at dancing hip-hop. Pravashni's mother had drugs issues and fell pregnant when she was a teenager. Pravashni has a little brother whose name is Dillon and they live with their grandparents. Pravashni has great talent, she sings, acts and dances very well. You are no where compared to her in singing, because you are shy. She beats you in music and acting.

You and Pravashni spend more time together. She wanted to lose weight three months ago and you wanted to do the splits. It's your dream to be able to do the splits. You both decided to do aerobics. You were afraid to tell anyone in the class because you knew they were all going to laugh at you. According to most people your age, that's the place to go to for losing weight. When your classmates found out, they laughed at you and your size, most girls said, "Aerobics is going to make you skinnier than you already are, you're going to disappear, aaaa haha ha!" Pravashni said, "Saesha don't listen to them, if you like aerobics than that shouldn't be their business."

The school has transport for those who joined MDDActive. You both meet with other students in your school who joined MDDActive. There you meet a far cousin of yours. She is close family to family from your mother's side. You get along well with her. You can't believe she's so open minded compared to other family members on your mother's side. On the way to MDDActive, you all get along. You find out more about her, some things that you know your aunty won't be very happy about if she finds out. She's worried that you will spy her out to her aunty. You don't think that what she's doing is such a big deal anyway, and besides you normally keep information to yourself. To make her feel better you say, "Don't worry I won't spy you out. It's not a big deal, I eat meat." She says, "Oh! Ok, don't worry I won't tell your aunty."

Sometimes you want to dodge school. Dodging school isn't difficult. Since you are at school most days, your mum doesn't mind if you hang around at home. One day Pravashni joins you because she can't go to her house. You and Pravashni manage to make it to Virsha's school just before break time. Virsha often tells you where she usually hangs out during breaktime. As she comes out, she sees you by the fence. She says, "Hey Saesha, wait here, I'll get us some chiprolls." Chiprolls are small rolls filled with spiced french fries and sauce. You split your roll with Pravashni. It's very common to receive chip rolls on sport days. You can't believe how nice Virsha is to look after you and Pravashni.

In one subject at school you are all put in pairs and have to come up with something fun to show the class. Then the class has to pick the winner from the two groups. The teacher gives you dates and tells you which groups will present their ideas on which day. Asika finds out that the other group is planning to do an Indian dance, and she decides to do an English dance. She comes to you and asks you for help, because she knows you can dance, and wants you to teach her group some steps. They choose a song from the group two unlimited, the song "No limits." You teach them the steps, and the dance comes out really cool. Asika tells you, "Saesha vote for me to win." You don't say anything because you know with your steps they are going to win. She puts most of the class against the other group. It seems like most of the class doesn't like the other group. She even tells a girl from the other group, "Saesha is throwing a party and she's not inviting you." You see half the class side with Asika, and Asika asks you to pretend that you are going to throw a party and that you are not inviting them. You do it after seeing how many people are on Asika's side and you say to yourself, "There must be reasons why people don't like the other group." A girl from the other group doing the Indian dance comes to you and says, "Saesha, I hear you're

throwing a party and not inviting me. Please invite me."
You answer coldly, "I don't know, I'll see." Everyone
waits for the day that Asika would face the other group.
She prepares everyone to vote for them, and they agree
to do it. You vote for them, because you taught them
the steps and like the dance, which you taught them.
That day Asika won again, and the other group feels
really bad. They know that the winning was planned.

During breaks, you hardly hang around with Chameli
and Hasini. You see Juhi at times too. She now is at the
same high school as you, in fact she is in Standard
eight.

What do you know about love!

Maxwell and Virsha often meet up in a park in front of Maxwell's house. You also meet them and hang out together. Virsha doesn't shout at Maxwell a lot these days. She used to get upset and complain to you about how she hated it when Maxwell asked her permission to kiss or hold her hand. During school holidays, you and Virsha get calls from Delta Spar, they sometimes ask you both to come to work only when they're understaffed. When they call Virsha, Virsha often says, "Can I call you back in a few minutes?" Normally they say, "Ok" and then Virsha calls you to find out if Delta Spar called you too. This way you both plan your answers. When you both don't feel like going to work, you can both make excuses. You spend your free time on Fridays playing pool or just hanging out together. The click is now bigger. While playing pool you all sing and sometimes dance to the music which is playing. You and Virsha go mad when you hear the songs, *All that she wants*, *Wheel of fortune*, and *Living in danger*. Right now Ace of Base is your favourite band. Maxwell's best friend often hangs around with you and his name is Dean. Maxwell and Virsha are getting very serious in their relationship. Somedays when Dean isn't around you all go to Maxwell's house and hang out in his room. He shuts the door to have his privacy with his friends or if he is with Virsha.

Eventually you start getting bored at Maxwell's house. You always end up sitting on the floor watching Maxwell and Virsha kissing on the bed forever. One day they get busy, until you have enough. You head straight for the door and walk out of the house. At least four minutes go by when you see Maxwell running behind you. After that day, you never have to sit on the floor in the room, watching them kiss like they did before.

At least two months passes after that incident and Maxwell decides to hook you up with Dean. Dean is a real nice person, but you are not attracted to him. However, you never hear a soul saying anything bad about him. Everyone who knows Dean makes you see how special he is. It is for that reason that you decide to go out with Dean but don't have any feelings for him. "What does anyone know about love at the age of 14", you often say. You tell Maxwell casually one day, "I don't think Dean is *thee* guy," and somehow it ends without you both saying anything to each other officially. You and Dean last 3 months; you never called each other and meet up only when you're with Maxwell and Virsha. You think, "Well perhaps it's for the best when I can count on one hand the number of times I've seen him in a month." Now Maxwell and Virsha keep breaking up and getting back together.

It is the festival of lights and there's a fireworks display at The Hindu Samaj. Maxwell and Virsha decide to come along. You see someone who you liked when you were little, you say in your mind, "Oh my God! It's Vinesh!" The first thing that comes to your mind is the day you went to leave the books the teacher gave you at his house. You remembered going up the stairs with the books. You heard someone singing, and it sounded like him. You followed his voice and came to a room. You ended up standing right in front of the bathroom, and your mouth dropped. He had his jockey on while he was showering. It wasn't odd to shower or bath in your underwear when most of yous were young. You remember seeing him dancing in the shower while he sang. He turned around and saw you standing there. He smiled and put one hand across his groin covering his private parts and with the other hand; he stretched slightly for the door and swung it closed in style. He tried singing after that but his voice sounded uncomfortable.

Now he is tall, thin, and still has the same face. His hair is black and short like the old days. You wonder if you have a chance with him now that you are older. You're more stylish than before. You get Virsha's and Maxwell's attention. You tell them, "Ok don't look there to make it obvious." They almost turn and you say, "No, No look there after a while. You see there, that boy over there..." and point slightly to his direction, "I used to like him when I was little." Maxwell and Virsha look after a while and Maxwell says with determination, "Right I'm going to speak to him." You are in shock, and don't know if it's a good idea, but then you say to Maxwell, "Ok it's worth a try." Maxwell goes over and introduces himself and after a while, you and Virsha see him looking in your direction. Maxwell is trying to set you both up. Funny enough, he doesn't do a bad job. Now and again, in the beginning, you call each other, but you call more than he calls you and never see each other because he is studying in a private school and comes home late.

Now Abhay calls Shalini a waste so often that it irritates you. You defend her and shout back at Abhay, "You are a waste! You left school! You smashed the car." One day your dad brings home "The Colt." Your father's boss gives him the Colt somedays. It's an automatic car and it's an ugly green colour. Sometimes Vivek wants to drive it, and your father goes with him. Vivek says "It's easy." One Saturday Virsha comes to your house. Shalini says to you father, "Can I drive the Colt?" Your father says, "Ok, after lunch." You, Virsha and your mum also want to go. You all jump in. Your father tells her what to do. You all go in the direction of the temple. Things are going smoothly. You and Virsha say, "Wow, she is driving!" Your father says, "Ok, Shalini now turn right, just here." Shalini gets nervous after seeing a car behind her from the rear view mirror and then sees one coming to the stop sign on the road where your father is asking her to turn. She's not turning the wheel. You all know if she doesn't turn and turns too late she'll hit the other car waiting at the stop sign, or she has to decide to continue straight. Shalini is turning and straightening the wheel, she doesn't know if she must turn or go straight. You, Virsha, and your father panic you all scream, "Turn! Turn!" she takes a quick sharp turn, the car is out of control, and she's not straightening the wheel. If she keeps the wheel there, you are all going to crash into the cars parked in front of the temple. You and Virsha close your eyes, you know you are going to crash, she holds the wheel there without straightening it, and now the car's taking a sharp turn, you think you are all going to die and finally the car stops aggressively. Shalini was extremely lucky, she managed to get straight into a parking spot between two cars. It was sheer luck, if not the Colt could have been finished. You and Virsha jump out, you say, "Wow! I'm not getting into the car with you again if you're driving!"

154

It's Spring day, you meet Mark and Cris in the assembly area at school. You see them with the music teacher who sometimes comes with you all to MDDActive. You and Pravashni presume that they will do a show for the school event on spring day. You and Pravashni are not popular girls, but when you both speak with Mark and Cris everyone looks at you both with interest. You think, "Surely they're wondering what two coloured boys are doing in an Indian school." Mark and Cris leave an incredible performance for the Spring day show that takes place in the assembly area. MDDActive is now over and the dance that you and Pravashni practice for at MDDActive was for a big stage concert, which already took place. It was really cool to do a dance with electronic music. Your parents couldn't come because there was no car. Now, there's an audition for a role in Jesus Christ Superstar and Pravashni gets one of the main roles, she also starts dating a guy. You both spend less time together. She goes to practice for her role in Jesus Christ Superstar and hangs out with her boyfriend. He comes and picks her up after gym.

It's close to the end of the year. At work, Virsha and Mitali are getting closer. Virsha tells you that she and her family are going to move to Johannesburg and that she is going to go to the same school as Mitali. Mitali is excited. You are absolutely happy for both of them because you all get along quite well. You think, "At least Virsha is going to have a good friend." At the end of 1993, Virsha moves with her family to Johannesburg, and you are happy for them. It seems that they've overcome this problem and have become closer as a family. It also works out well in your favour.

Once you bumped into Prenesan and Virsha's mother while you were with Virsha and her sister. You didn't want to see him again, but when you saw him, you hated him more and more. You didn't want anymore situations like that again.

It's starting to kick in

During the school holidays your life starts changing. Virsha is now gone. After the incident with Prenesan, you feel sick and seem to hate men more and more. If you are the only girl sitting in the salon between your father and brother you feel sick and hate them. You start feeling depressed and hardly have any friends. You try to call a children's helpline to ask for help about certain issues. When you call the number and ask the operator if you can speak to a social worker, the operator asks you, "Tell me what's the problem." You don't know how to say it, and build the courage to say it and say quickly, "I've been molested." You feel embarrassed after saying it. The operator says, "I don't believe you, this is a prank," and hangs up. You think to yourself, "After all it took to say it, she doesn't even believe me." You try to solve the issue yourself.

A few months go by and things are hard for you. You can't stand your father and your brothers at times. You get angry with them even though they did nothing to you. You think about telling someone at home. You don't want to tell Shalini because you know she doesn't know how to handle it, and she won't even know what the word "molest" is. You try asking Vivek what you should do. One day, when he is alone in the salon you approach him. You ask, "Do you know the word molest?" He says, "Yes." You say, "I think it happened to me." He says jokingly, "Ooo A man touched you and your tits..." he is about to go further, but the way he says it makes you feel disgusted with yourself, and you walk away. This makes you dislike Vivek even more, you tell yourself, "It's clear that I have to do this alone,

157

I can't count on anyone here, I am on my own and I am going to face this alone." Any television ads or films that have small scenes of caressing or kissing makes you feel uncomfortable. When those scenes last longer than a minute you get up discreetly and act as if you have to do something, and leave the salon. This is common in your house. Your mother does it all the time. Sometimes you don't even want to sit with everyone in the salon, and start to go into isolation. You sit mainly in front of the television when your sister is there, and can't rely on your mother because she does the same thing as you. You don't want to make it obvious that this makes you uncomfortable. Even in summer you dressed covered up and don't want to attract anyone from the opposite sex. You have mainly dark blue jeans and black tops. You can't stop crying at times. You look for privacy and let it out. You don't want to live anymore.

Your mum has a habit of storing things under the beds because she doesn't have enough space in the cupboards. She stores a lot of things and some things are stored for you and your sister's wedding. One day, as you cry you want to die so badly. You wish with all your soul. You look for something to kill yourself and find blades under your bed. They are for the kitchen, for making salads and cutting fruit and vegetables. You look for a less painful way to kill yourself. You want to do it quick and clean. You think of the pain you will feel if you don't get it right. You say, "Just imagine living with one hand or leg all my life. It's better not living at all. If I am going to do it than I have to make sure that I don't stay alive!" You take the blade, and try putting the knife into you and when it reaches your stomach, you try to push it in slowly. "Damn it's not sharp enough to just slice through," so you push the knife in further. This hurts, and you can't find the guts to do it. Then you decide to cut your hand so that you could die bleeding, and change your mind and tell yourself, "No the leg, this will empty the blood out of my body quicker." You try cutting your leg, and it burns and hurts. You now have a small cut, and it's hurting like hell. You finally decide on cutting yourself little by little everyday. Since the blade is right under your bed, you take it out when you're depressed. The days you'd feel very depressed you'd have more motivation to cut yourself a little more. This works for you and as the days go by you tolerate the pain and cut further than the day before. Your leg has a deep cut now, and it hurts a lot. You've been doing this for at least three weeks until one day the blades disappear. You figure it's for the best and think, "What if I survive the suicide, than I won't have a leg left," so you quit with this idea of killing yourself. Your depression hits you so often, that you just want to be alone. Your mind isn't at rest, and the things that happened with Virsha's father repeats and takes you back to that day. You didn't think that being molested for such a brief time can cause all this.

One day you take what you feel out on paper. You write:

" Looking back
Fresh tears roll down my eyes one ahead of the other.
Eyes staring in one direction with remembrance of the painful day.
The day that could change ones' life forever.

159

Walls staring back at me,
so still can't move, helpless as I was then.
Only they don't feel yet listen, and see everything but
can't say or do a thing.
One tear running faster than the others.
Running away and living faster than maximum,
can't even slow down to minimum.
You'd never thought you'd never feel,
until the day comes for real."

Chameli now has a boyfriend. One day, you see
Chameli and her friends hanging out at their
grandmother's house. They call you over when they see
you outside. As you enter their house, you find one of
Chameli's friends with a cigarette. She tells you, "If
you want to hang around with us you must smoke a
cigarrette." She's offering you a cigarrette. You take
one, and someone lights it up for you. You take a puff
and quickly let it out. The girl says strictly, "No! Take a
puff and hold it in for long." You take a puff and try
holding it for long, and you let out a suffocating cough.
You leave your cigarette in the ashtray and walk out of
Chameli and Juhi's house. You tell yourself, "Who
needs friends like this?"

On hot days Bhajia's "pink lipstick" often sticks out of
his Scrotal Sac. Shalini makes fun of him and calls
Bhajia's penis "pink lipstick." Bhajia has a very short
tail. Anuj Kaka had to cut Bhajia's tail after he was in
an accident. His tail has been infected ever since.
Bhajia always runs in circles chasing his short tail when
it itches. He goes in circles trying to bite it and at times
gets angry at it and starts barking at it. One day your
mum tells you to go and buy some tomatoes. You come

back with the tomatoes and just as you enter the kitchen, a tomato falls out of the bag. Bhajia runs for it and eats it in seconds. You are surprised. You know that Bhajia is vegetarian but didn't know that he likes tomatoes too. So, whenever you eat something you give some of it to Bhajia to see if he also likes it, strange enough Bhajia even likes bananas. Bhajia hates dried dog chunks; he likes juicy, meaty canned dog food.

One evening you're bored looking at Bhajia eating while feeding him. You often provoke Bhajia. It's Friday night, two days before the end of your school holidays. You have a long stick in your hand and while Bhajia eats you think of doing something very naughty to provoke him. You have a stick in your hand. You stretch out your hand so that the stick touches Bhajia's scrotal sac. You push it and sway it sidewards. Bhajia starts growling and swallowing at the same time. It sounds pretty funny to you, and you chuckle. You try it again, and he growls even longer and a little louder, you chuckle even louder. You decide to stop and pet him to say sorry. You go closer, and sit down near him to pet him. As you get closer and stretch your hand out to pet him, he turns and bites your lip so hard that it starts to bleed. After he bites you, he looks scared and you too are scared. Bhajia never bites, actually he is a very shy, friendly, and quiet dog. You run to the mirror, and the blood doesn't stop running. Your lip is swollen, you wonder about Vinesh's sister who is going to start high school on Monday. You were planning to impress her and show her how cool you are. You imagine the scene and say, "Damn, now I am not going to look cool with my lip like this. Going to school with a fat swollen lip on the first day is going to be embarrassing. Every one

161

is going to laugh at me!" You quickly go to Shalini and show her what happened. She laughs when you tell her how it happened. It is 10 o'clock at night and you both go looking for a doctor. Two streets down you find a doctor who is about to close. He allows you and Shalini in. He takes a look at it and says, "You might need stitches for that." He asks, "How did it happen?" You are embarrassed to tell him and just leave it as, "My dog bit me." He repeats, "You need to go to a hospital to get stitches." You ask, "Do you have something that I can use to stop it from getting infected?" He gives you something. You don't want stitches; you are scared of it and say to yourself, "If I get stitches I'm going to look ridiculous on Monday." Two days gone, and your lip is less swollen and it just has a cut, which is visible. You are relieved, but still hide away on Monday.

Standard Seven

You stop going to aerobics. Now that Virsha is gone, you think perhaps you can still be friends with Maxwell and hang around with him. You visit Maxwell sometimes but it feels odd. Sometimes you see Dean with Maxwell. He is taller and much more handsome than before. You feel like you missed out. You tell Maxwell to call you and ask him to pass the message to the others to meet up but none of Virsha's old friends contact you. You and Virsha call each other. You visit Maxwell at times, but it's a short visit, because you both don't know what to talk about, and that's where the friendship stayed. At times, it feels odd meeting up with Maxwell alone. Maxwell calls Virsha at times and he misses her. Virsha calls Maxwell too.

You and Pravashni continue with MDDActive. The far cousin from your mother's side doesn't join this year. You see her sometimes at school. Some months go by and you find her picture in the newspaper. She is married to the man. Your aunty and her family are looking for her, and the guy who she married is much older than her they say. This is pretty common and it's not the first time that someone ran away from home to get married or to be with their boyfriend. Once the parents of a girl came looking for her at your house. Shalini's friend told Shalini not to tell anyone that she is going to run away with the guy. She even told Shalini where she could find her. Shalini didn't want to tell her parents anything. You remember telling Shalini that she should tell them the truth. Shalini told her parents eventually where they could find their daughter.

There is a girl in your class that comes from a Muslim family. She likes the principle's son and tries to get his attention. She lives close to you and one day she comes to school wearing a short skirt. She tells you all the next day that her father came to the shops and slapped her in front of everyone for wearing a short skirt. She tells you "I'm going to run away from home." You don't advise her, because you know how parents can be around here with their kids. She tells you and other classmates, "If my parents come looking for me say you know nothing." Her parents come to your house to look for her. Now you see the pressure Shalini felt when her friend ran away. You tell them what you know. You find out that their parents eventually find her, but she stops coming to school.

One day from all the depression and crying over the incident that marked your life with Virsha's stepfather you say, "What's all this crying for? Stop feeling sorry for yourself, get up and be a strong girl." Ever since, you don't cry about the incident again. When it comes to you, you push it out of your memory. You do this constantly.

One day, Virsha calls and asks, "Hey Saesha, my parents are coming to visit some family. They are going to be there the whole day. Can I hang around with you the whole day?" You're excited to see her and say, "Of course." When Virsha comes she says, "Let's go see Maxwell." You say, "Ok, it's been a long time since I've seen him too." Maxwell really misses Virsha and is happy to see her. You arrive at the park while Virsha goes to Maxwell. You sit on the swing in front of Maxwell's house and give them privacy. Virsha calls you, you come and she says to Maxwell, "Maxwell, call Seasha and get the others to meet up like we all used to do." Maxwell says, "Ok." You know Maxwell will not call. You both leave but Maxwell doesn't come along.

Abhay is sick of his job in the market. He decides to leave and look for a new job. He has sinusitis. He even decides to buy a car from a Police auction. You are all excited. The car arrives and it's not what you all expect. It's missing some front lights, the engine starts but the car is a mess inside. Actually, inside it stinks like hell, and there are lots of trash inside it. Abhay says, "I am going to do up the engine and then sell it for more than what I bought it for." You help Abhay clean the car. Your father laughs and says, "The car is missing some eyes, and ears." It was a real job to clean this car.

Standard eight

It's 1994 Shalini finishes high school, she doesn't know what to study. You push her to go to a real College to study. Your father is willing to pay the cost for whatever she wants to study. Abhay now consistently calls her a waste. She doesn't say anything and does nothing to defend herself. This makes you angry yet she still continues to do everything that Abhay asks of her.

It is time for you to choose a course. You never did pass Mathematics and don't pass now, you are also average in Science. To study an important field in University depends on Maths and Science marks. You are into Art, Biology, Geography, Typing and everything else that doesn't require counting. For those who don't like Mathematics and Science, or for those who didn't pass them or didn't want to take it up, there are not a lot of options. You really want to do Art and find it so stupid that you could only have six subjects and that the course that had Art is with Mathematics and Science. You don't want to do the loafers course, but you are in that class now for the time being. Juhi failed Standard 8 and she too is in your class. The daughter of a Muslim man a few houses where Abhay threw fireworks some years ago is also in your class. You decide to take up the Secretarial course, the same course that Shalini took up. The principle tells you, "You have to be a lot in a class for us to run that course." You try to find other girls to join the course. You manage to get enough people to join your course, and they are mainly girls. At the end, you stay in what everyone calls the loafer's course; a losers course. Now you begin to learn about Shakespeare.

You get an Afrikaans teacher, who is a "Hare Krishna" follower. His head is almost shaved, yet he has one long strand of hair. It looks like a pigtail. "Sikha" is the name referred to this strand of hair. Doing this is some kind of personal sacrifice to god. It is also said that "Krishna" is part of an ancient Sanskrit epic based on facts. There is a Hare Krishna Temple in Johannesburg that you once went to with Virsha's family. It is common to see the Hare Krishna movement where devotees wear orange and some men wear orange dhotiyus. In fact, your Afrikaans teacher wore an orange dhotiyu to school. Now it's a habit to call him among you all "Hare Krishna Teacher." Some Muslim people in your class frown when they see him for the first time. At school, it's normal to see classmates forming groups. It's common to find groups of Hindus together, groups of Muslims together, while Christians and Tamils create a group among themselves.

Now you are tired of Delta Spar. It's boring there, and the pay is low for the work you are doing. Virsha doesn't come on Fridays anymore, and you work alone on Fridays. When you see Virsha and Mitali on Saturdays, you feel completely out, only between them they know what they're talking about. You are lost. Sometimes they even stop coming to work on the weekends. You are working hard and doing their work too. You have time for nothing and it's too much work for you. You decide to leave Delta Spar. Shalini wants to take your place to work there. You organize it for her. You don't understand why Shalin's studies are so flexible, but than again you are not convinced that she's doing something serious for her life. She starts working at Delta Spar doing your job.

Shalini is studying fashion designing at a house. It doesn't convince you. She says she's going to get a good certificate and it's cheap. You wonder, "This sounds familiar. Cheap shouldn't be a choice for your future. You hope Shalini is going to make something of her life unlike Abhay" You tell her, "You should have chosen a College where you can learn a lot more and get a better professional qualification than to just learn fashion designing in a house." She gets upset with you.

At school, you are having fun. Making friends again is easy. A new girl joins your class, and you make friends with her so that she has someone to hang around with during break times. It is also easy for Juhi to make friends. You both needed each other. Others, who don't have a group to hang around with, hang with you and Juhi. You often laugh in your mind and call yourself or your group, "The rejects." It seems as if no one wants to be with any one of you. The Hare Krishna Teacher makes easy exams, so passing Afrikaans isn't a problem. The Hare Krishna Teacher is fun and treats everyone fair. One day you bring some "mag" to school. "Mag" is the Gujarati word for "Mung bean." In Afrikaans, you all misbehave and the Hare Krishna Teacher allows it. You take a bic pen out in Afrikaans class, and take out the disposable ink. You put the mung bean in the hole of the tube were the disposable was and look for someone who you know will take this as a joke. Juhi is watching you and is shaking her head. You know that sign of hers. It's the one that says don't do it, you're going to get into trouble. You blow hard from the other end of the pen and the mung bean flies in the air until it finally hits the person. You quickly put your pen down, turn and face the teacher like nothing

168

happened. Juhi can't believe that you just did that. You look from the side of your eye and the person who you just hit with the bean seems a little confused. Some are observing what you're doing and find it funny. You do this to a few more people, and your classmates start asking you for mung beans. Now the whole class is shooting each other and there's mung all over the floor. Someone shoots the teacher while someone in the class screams, "Someone is shooting mung!" The teacher bends down to pick up the mung that hit him, and now you are worried, he looks at you all and says with a smile, "Who brought this mung?" Everyone points to you laughing and the teacher says, "Saesha you must sweep the class afterwards." Everyone starts to laugh even more and you say in your mind, "Shoooooo, it could have been worse." You say loudly, "Ok, I will."

You and Juhi hang around at times after school. Juhi is dating Chameli's boyfriend's best friend. They hide and see their boyfriends because their father doesn't know. You meet up with them sometimes. One day Juhi tells you she's anaemic. You ask her, "What's that?" and she says, "My blood is too thin, but I take some tablets for it."

There is a boy in your class that repeats Standard 8 for the second time. He is older than all of you and failing Standard 8 twice isn't the first time for him. He ends up in a fight with the Hare Krishna teacher one day. He looked for a fight because he has issues with religion. Hindu's and Muslims generally have conflict with each other in your town. One day Vivek ends up in a fight after school at Gina's Cafe. Gina's Cafe is a tiny shop at the corner of your street near to your school. When

Vivek comes home, his hair is a mess and his tie is over his shoulder, his shirt is hanging out of his trousers and some of his buttons are missing. You ask him what happened and he says, "A Sulla called me "Bania." The Hindus at school have a slang word for the Muslims. They often use the word "Sulla." In this case, a Muslim guy called Vivek "A Bania." A word used to tease Vivek for being a vegetarian. Even vegetarians among the Hindus that eat meat are given a name. Usually it's not a very positive one. You remember some people calling Abhay a "Mag." Some of your friends call you "Mag" too referring to the Mung bean. Mung beans are one of many staple diets in the state of Gujarat, India; therefore, it's commonly used in Gujarati cuisine.

You wonder about Priya, and think how similiar the situations are with Devi Masi's family. Devi Masi has a lot of daughters and just one son. You think, "It's unfair for rich families to give their sons private education while they send their daughters to public school."

It's February 14, 1994. You see Vinesh's sister Priya at school and greet her. Priya is very beautiful. She has long straight hair, which reaches her butt. Her hair is shiny, and she's fair. She looks like a bollywood actress. Her eyes are medium in width and long. She has very brown eyes. You think of an idea and want to give Vinesh a Valentines present. At school you wonder what you can give since it's last minute. Priya normally passes your house when she's on her way to and from school. When the bell rings, you speed home like "Road Runner," you can't stop and talk today and tell yourself, "If anyone comes in my way I will "Beep Beep." "Road Runner" is an animation series. You want

170

to be the first one to get home from school and speed past the first of those coming out of the school gate. You have an idea and know that Priya is still far from passing your house. You rush home and take the Valentines present that Vivek got last year from some girl. You inspect it for a second and say to yourself, "Hmmm, It looks in good condition, and just needs to be dusted from the one year that it has been standing on your family's shelf." You have no idea what it is, it is red and looks like a typical Valentines gift. You have this ... this green looking teddy bear that you won from a machine in some shop, which looks new, and quickly shove it on this thing and look for some sweets to put on it. Shalini laughs at it. It looks pretty good. It is a good size too, and off it goes. You look through the window and wait for a few minutes. You see Priya passing the house. You shoot out and say, "Hey Priya, can I give you something to give to Vinesh for Valentines Day". She says, "Yes," you shoot back in to the house and bring out the green and red looking thing.

Sometimes Juhi calls you to her house, and before you go, you buy some sweet and sour dry fruit snacks to eat at their house. Your town has a rich variety of snacks. One in particular that you love is "Sour figs." You just love them. At Gina's cafe, they sell sweet and sour dry plums, sour figs, other things that come from your courntry, China, and India. The sour fig is a fruit that grows in South Africa. Another name for it is the "Hottentot Fig." It doesn't need a lot of soil, but needs a lot of sun and usually grows along the coast. The fruit contains succulent pulp. The word "Hottentot" is a word Dutch settlers gave to the KhoiKhoi. The KhoiKhoi's are one of two Koisan ethnic groups. The other group is "San." It is said that the San people inhabited South Africa first. Years later came European settlers. Another favourite fruit you love is "Bora," a berry, which grows in India. In your town, it's known as Bor. You don't like chocolates and sweet stuff. In fact as a child your favourite snack were crisps, but lately it's crisps, and these South Africa, Chinese and Indian snacks. They sell them dry or sometimes with various sweet and sour sauces. In India, "Bora" grows freely and children pick them on their way to school, and love eating it with salt. Bora is rich in vitamins and has many medicinal benefits. At home, you were all taught to share with others, and if there's only one of it left, it must be shared and at times even given away. You and your siblings don't apply this among each other, but apply it to your cousins, friends, uncles and aunties. Sometimes it makes you mad to be so generous when not everyone is like your family, however it's a habit with you. When you visit Juhi, you share what you have with her and her sister. They love it.

Elections are coming, and people are going crazy. It's getting closer to April. You don't understand what the people are panicking about. Everyone is saying that Mandela is going to be the president of South Africa. Your sister laughs and tells you, "You said that Mandela was the president one day, now it's going to be true." People think that the country is going to go down. You don't know anything about politics and say to yourself, "Can it really be that bad?" In your town, people are talking about buying loads of food products and storing them just in case things get worse, others are saying that many White South Africans are planning to leave South Africa. You wonder how other countries

172

work. The television channels don't put a lot of things about other countries, and you assume that other countries are like South Africa. You say to yourself, "If things are hard everywhere, how will they be if it gets worse here? It's already hard as it is." You worry about your future and pray for your country not to go down.

Some time passes, Vinesh and you talk now and again, but he never asks to meet up with you and he never calls. You see a guy called Manav hanging around in your area. He hangs around with some guys you know randomly. You observe him one day, he lies on the grass with his hands behind his head, something about his way doesn't attract you and you say to yourself, "How can anyone like this kind of guy. There's just no way that I'll be attracted to this kind of guy. Wait a minute why the hell am I thinking about this?"

Vivek's going to India. He is going with Sita Masi's son. Sita Masi's son comes and picks him up for school every morning. Since he passes your house, he stops at your place and goes with Vivek. Vivek, your cousin, your aunty and uncle are going to India. In India, they will meet up with Kalpana Masi. You wonder, "Why do Vivek and Sita Masi's son get to go? Why can't Shalini and I join them?" Your father doesn't seem to have a problem with it. You think, "It's really unfair how he automatically gives your brothers what they want, yet thinks about your requests and hardly ever answers you."

At school, the guy who is the oldest in class makes his group of friends. Pravashni's group all seem to be more mature and serious. One from there is a mother and her boyfriend and Pravashni's boyfriend are best friends. You and Pravashni still get along well even though she has her own group. The oldest guy in your class starts to bully others. He tries and intimidates you and others in your class, but only tries it on those that don't put up a fight and guess what? You are one of those. He comes to your desk with his group of friends and sometimes picks on Juhi, or you or someone else in your group. He sometimes put his hand around your neck so tight that it makes you scared and stiff. This is his way of joking.

Mandela is now oficially the President of South Africa. There's a lot of movement in your country. People are talking about Mandela releasing prisoners who committed crimes from Robben Island. From all the movement going on you are learning a lot about your country. Robben Island is an Island close to Cape Town where many political prisoners are being held. Mandela too spent years there in prison. You wonder to yourself, "Why was Mandela in prison?" You have many questions and try to understand what is going on.

Abhay gets a new job. Shalini still gets teased "Olive," even though she's not in school anymore, and at home Abhay repeatedly calls her "A Waste." The fact that she is allowing Abhay to call her what he wants to call her is also irritating you. At home, you don't all eat together. There are no rules and everyone comes and eats when they want, Abhay expects Shalini to serve him at any time, sometimes he even wakes her up from her sleep to serve him. He's a real nuisance when he comes home late at night a little drunk. You get angry and tell Shalini, "Shalini don't serve him, he will get used to it, and make a habit of it, than he'll even expect

174

me to do it for him." Shalini ignores you. The more this happens the angrier you get with Abhay and Shalini. You tell him to stop it, and Shalini makes you angry because she does everything he asks of her. You say to yourself, "There's no point teaching him if she's going to do it for him all the time." Sometimes if Shalini isn't there he asks your mum to make his food hot. You can't believe he is so selfish. You wonder why your father doesn't say or do anything.

It's a long time since you spoke to Virsha. The last time you saw her was when she was with some older guys. In fact Virsha was dating one of them. She tells you, "One day I went into Johannesburg with friends and was surrounded by a few men, I was going to scream for help but one of them gave me such a look and had a cigarette close to my hand and threatened to burn me in case I scream. They robbed me." You know that Johannesburg is getting dangerous.

One day someone two streets away from you invites Shalini to a house party. Shalini takes you with her. It's been some time since you have danced. You are in fact dying to dance. At the party you meet all the people who you think are cool. You see Vivek with his gang of friends. In Vivek's gang there's a boy who failed the loafer's course and will end up in your class next year because he has to repeat. Viveks's gang make a circle, and the circle gets bigger. You see some people from Vivek's group showing off their steps. You and Shalini go there. You see the boy from Vivek's gang who is going to be in your class next year since he has to repeat. He is inside the circle. You know he is a very good dancer. After he finished showing his steps another guy goes in and shows his steps. The music is your confidence. All the songs that are playing here you already know and danced to before. You calculate the timing and you see others running out of steps. You wonder to yourself, "Should I, or shouldn't I? I might make a fool out of myself." The guy who is going to be in your class next year still hasn't run out of steps. He's in the circle right now, you wait, and you wait and doubt yourself and just than the chorus starts and the guy finishes, and "Bang" you shoot straight in.

So baby if you want me...

Everyone is in shock they didn't expect it, but you go straight in with the music like it should be. The super dancer is coming out again. Shalini is flipping and didn't think you'd be capable of doing it: Front, back, release, and front, back, release.

You've gotta show me love...

Now hold, drop, and touch down.

Words are so easy to say oh ah yeah...

The palm of your hand hits the ground and you rise up spinning like a top. The circle gets bigger because everyone wants to see what the big "Wow" is about.

You've gotta show me love...

Aaaaaaannd attitude! You give a teaser and leave everyone dumb. Some people who know you look at you in surprise. You wonder to yourself, "A lot of people didn't expect this tonight and neither did I!" You continue but try not to show off. Vivek and Shalini are in shock that you can dance this well. Now only you and the guy who will be in your class next year don't seem to run out of steps. It's like he's competing with you but you say to yourself, "It's all in your mind." You continue to enjoy yourself. After going for almost 30 minutes the guy runs out of steps and everyone tells him, "She beat you outright!" You think to yourself, "Did I hear right, I beat him outright," and realize it's been a competition all along, but you enjoyed yourself and won just by enjoying yourself. You feel free today, freer than ever. At the end of the party Shalini asks, "Saesha where did you learn all this?" You say, "In the salon when nobody is around." You hope that the boy you won at dancing wins you points at school since everyone thinks he is cool. You think, "He might tell everyone how well you can dance." When you arrive to school, you don't see the guy and eventually find out that he left school.

One day Shalini tells you, "Virsha and Mitali ran away from home. She said she found out at work." You are shocked and when they're found, Virsha and Shariksha move to Durban. Virsha calls you at times and you find out that they are living with their grandmother in Durban, still you don't know the whole story. The opposite neighbour says, "Stay away from Virsha, she's bad company." You don't know whether Mitali is the bad one, or if they're both just as bad.

During the holidays Juhi and Chameli's father finds out Chameli has a boyfriend, he also finds out that Juhi has a boyfriend. He orders Juhi not to see her boyfriend anymore. He says, "I knew his father, and he was an alcoholic." Juhi says to her father, "He doesn't drink." Her father says, "I don't care, you stop seeing him!" Juhi breaks up with him, but loves him a lot. She finds it hard and because of this Jayesh, who is Chameli's boyfriend doesn't know how to handle the situation. He loves Chameli and he is very close to his best friend. Juhi goes along with them everywhere, and Jayesh's best friend comes with him where he goes. Things get really bad with Juhi and her boyfriend, that Jayesh ends up in the middle. Jayesh gets angry and says, "I don't want him in my car." Juhi tells her boyfriend this and Jayesh loses his friend. Juhi asks you to come along with them wherever they go. You discover places with them, and enjoy hanging around with them. You all go to the cinema together, something you hardly do. You look forward to go out with them. In the beginning, you think they're not going to show up, since people had the habit of including you in their plans then changing it last minute, somedays they come late but never disappoint you. Eventually you all become great friends. Hasini and Chameli don't hang around together a lot these holidays. You stopped eating meat years ago. You only ate meat now and again with Virsha. After the cow vomitting incident, you never touch meat again. You are curious to try wine when Chameli and Juhi order it. You don't like it at all. Jayesh says, "It takes a bit of time to get used to it."

You decide to give your father a surprise party. You invite Sita Masi's family; she is close to your mum. Her son, who use to pick up Vivek in the mornings finished high school with Vivek. Now he will study at a University while Vivek decides to study at a College.

All the family on your dad's side live far away. Your cousins from Sita Masi's family don't come with their parents, so the party is small, turns out well and finishes early. Abhay has the habit of avoiding family. He never wants to see them or go to any family functions. You are all already used to it so you expect that he's not going to join the little party for his father from the beginning.

Now that Vivek is going to College, it's his turn to get called a waste, but the word that Abhay uses on him a lot is "Lity," which is negative and means "Kid." Vivek keeps his will power, and tries not to waste his energy on Abhay, as Abhay can really provoke someone. It seems that Abhay starts to put anyone in the house down who is close to finishing high school. He puts you down, but still not that much, probably it's not your turn yet, but when your turn comes, you say, "I'll be ready for him."

Standard Nine

It's 1995, now Sita Masi's youngest daughter comes to your house to pick you up for school. Chameli fails standard eight and has to repeat, while in your class there is a black student. You are surprised and look in her direction often, only because she's black. You always thought that since you are all Indians living in one area, you all went to the nearest school close to your house. Everyone in your class has the impression that black South africans are supposed to be stupid, until she beats most of you in a test. You think, "She must have really put an effort and surely it isn't easy being poor and black." You somehow have this impression that all black South africans are poor and wonder about her life for a bit.

Now this guy Manav is dating a girl and likes football. He has short black hair, and always wears a cap. He seems too confident of himself that you try not to get nervous. You haven't seen him around here a lot, until lately. He says Hi and bye to your brother and you see him on just on one or two occasions with Vivek and his friends. Something about him puts you off and you wonder to yourself, "Can he even have girls interested in him, he's just peculiar."

You have something close to a thousand rands saved up after working at Delta Spar. You don't know what to do with the money. Your birthday is coming up soon and you are going to be sixteen. Here turning sixteen is celebrated and you want to have a party with the money you saved up for yourself and your friends. You tell your idea to Jayesh, Chameli and Juhi and wonder if it's possible to have a party with that amount of money. Jayesh, Juhi, and Chameli help you with the cost planning and you all come to the conclusion that you are short of four hundred rands for the cases of coke. Someone in the class says he can sort out a DJ for cheap. You ask your father if he doesn't mind you having a birthday party with your own money. He doesn't answer you, so you don't know if you are allowed to or not. You try and get a response out of him, and you can only ask him for the four hundred rands if he says yes, but he isn't giving you an answer. You say, "I might need four hundred rands for the cases of coke but that's it, I have the rest covered." You wonder, "How difficult can it be to just say yes, I mean last year he paid a ticket to India for Vivek." His attitude frustrates you. He finally shakes his head as a sign of yes. You, Jayesh, Chameli and Juhi start planning the things for the party. You tell your brothers and sister that you are having a party. Abhay doesn't seem too keen, until you tell him, "I'm having it with my own money."

It's fun planning your own party, and it's working out cheap. You get the DJ for cheap because your classmate knows him. You calculate around one hundred people to invite. You, Juhi, Chameli, and Jayesh make the invites, but you don't have enough. Your plan is to tell neighbours and people nearby in person to come because you can save on invites. You even give your mother's side of the family invites. Everything is ready, and you call your cousins and tell them to come to the party. Some cousins from your father's side come and tell you what to do. You don't like it, and tell them nicely you have it organized. One in particular doesn't listen and asks with an unfriendly tone, "How many people are you inviting?" You say, "Around one hundred people." He says, "One hundred people won't fit in your yard." You know that many people can fit in your yard because it's really big. You have been to many house parties with Juhi, Chameli, and Jayesh and some houses were so small yet fit in so many people. The fact that your older cousin just walks into your house as if it's his and speaks to you as if you are stupid makes you angry. He doesn't ask about you, your plans, ideas and just starts to interfere. You tell him, "Just come to the party, everything is already organized."

It's Shalini's birthday, she's going to turn twenty one. You can't buy her anything because you spent all your money in the party. So far, when Abhay turned twenty one, she bought him a small present. She came home thinking she'll get at least a present or there'll be a cake, because twenty one is also a celebrated age. She's disappointed. It's pretty common to forget birthdays in your house, and basically you can expect not receiving anything on your birthday. Last year, only Shalini remembered your birthday, she told your mother, father, and your brothers and if you didn't tell everyone that it's Shalini's birthday, than they won't even know that her birthday even exists. It's only you and Shalini who remembers everyone's birthdays and it's Shalini who makes more effort than anyone in your house. You tell Shalini, "Well than, this party that I'm having, is also for you. We can celebrate together." This makes her happy.

It's Saturday, Vivek and his friends puts up the tent and are busy decorating it. They all seem excited. You,

Juhi, Chameli and Jayesh organize the last things needed for tonight. Everything is looking good and things look like they´re going to be on time. You hope your party isn't going to be a flop. Your father's side of the family comes early to help. You're okay with the fact that they want to help, but the fact that they are not respecting the way you and your friends planncd things makes you pretty angry. You have vegetarian and meat dishes with labels. It's that same cousin again who wants to have reason to meddle, and is always trying to help, instead of just having fun and letting things be. Abhay happened to be with you and your cousin insists, "Saesha you and Abhay must open the dance." Abhay screams out loud, "No way I'm out of here!" while you're busy screaming inside, "No way I can handle my brother touching me." Abhay was gone in a second. You're swearing at this cousin in your mind, "Look what you've done, now Abhay isn't going to hang around in the party." Your cousin asks another cousin to open the dance with you. You know that if the DJ puts on a fast number everyone will just start to dance, but now you are just so tired of fighting your cousin that you can't take anymore. You thought that blowing the candles was the first and last part of being the centre of attention in this party and just want to enjoy today with your friends and family. Opening the dance is nerve-wracking for you. You don't like being touched, but do it anyway. You open the dance with your cousin, and you sigh with relief to see the cousin who gets on your nerves joining the opening with his wife. After the opening, you go into the house and to the room you share with Shalini. You find four cousins in your room, all wearing something that belongs to you and your sister. They say, "We took this out of your cupboard, because everyone is dressed in jeans. We came with dresses on and don't feel comfortable in them." You say, "Okay no problem, come on I'll introduce you all to my friends."

Everyone enjoys themselves including your family. There seem to be more than 100 people, including some gatecrashes. You see Abhay enjoying himself too. You didn't expect him to be around and glad that he's here, because it means a lot to you. Family generally don't seem to matter to him that much. You look in a corner and see a couple kissing. You remember seeing them over an hour and they are still there kissing each other madly. The boy has her skirt right up to her thighs and his hands are roaming all over her legs. You look again, and realize it's Pravashni. You're shocked to see this side of her. Your mother's side of the family doesn't stick around for long, in fact they give you a present and leave, they didn't even eat anything. You don't expect presents, until Shalini shows you how many presents there are on the bed. You are shocked and you both shove them under the bed.

You invite some neighbours, but don't see them here. This Manav is hanging out with your brother and his friends. You were hungry in the beginning but with all the emotions, you eat nothing. You try to clear up a little so that there isn't a lot of work in the end. You check up on Bhajia, and he seems to be scared with so many people around. You have some empty coke bottles in your hand, but don't want to pass the crowd. A voice says, "Do you need some help?" You instantly want to say no, but you are also desperate to get the bottles over to the other side. An idea comes to your mind. You turn around and see Manav, you say, "Yes, can you pass me this bottle through this part of the gate while I go round to the other side to take it from you." He says, "Okay." When you get to the other side, he isn't there. You are quite disappointed, you go round again, and get the bottles yourself. Towards the end of the night, the DJ plays some slow music. Your cousins have already left. You can't stand slow dancing, and run from people who come and ask you to dance. It makes you feel very uncomfortable and nervous. You hate being touched especially by men, and in your home and generally in this culture showing affection in any way is not common, it makes you feel uncomfortable. Before running away again, you watch Manav dancing with his girlfriend and look at the way he holds her, he has her so close to him and runs his fingers through her hair. You find it really romantic and for a second you wish you were her. There's something pure about him right now. You realize that you're staring too much and tell yourself, "Saesha are you crazy thinking these things about this Manav. Look at him he has a girlfriend! Hello, he has a girlfriend!" You think about Vinesh and expect him to show up tonight, but he didn't. You wonder to yourself, "I don't even know if we are in a relationship, he never said so, I don't see him so much and we hardly talk on the phone. In fact it's a long time since we last spoke." The party ends and you all take the main things inside, and leave the rest of the work for tomorrow.

At school the boy who organized the DJ starts talking about your party, he says, "Your neighbours were looking through their window at your party, they were standing on something so that they can see. When we

185

saw them, we told the DJ, the DJ put the spotlight on their window. They all went down." You are surprised, and don't understand why they had to look at the party through the window and ask yourself, "Why didn't they come, they were invited?" You're daydreaming for weeks about this Manav, and wonder, "He was the only one, apart from my friends to offer me help during the party." You keep convincing yourself, "Come on Saesha, he didn't pass you the bottles at the end. He is a disappointment. How can you think good of him after that?" You get back to your senses, "After all he likes someone else, he's not going to like me when he's with someone else."

One day your class gets notified that another class will be joining you in common subjects like English, Biology, and Geography and than they'll separate when they have to go for Art, Science, and Mathematics. The new students join your class. You find one boy who is from Vivek's group of friends in your class. You think he'll make friends with you, or at least greet you, but he ignores you, and with him is this Manav.

Saturday nights is chips night at home. Every Saturday night you eat French fries for dinner. It's a habit to serve the males in the house first, that's if they are very hungry. Sometimes your sister or your mother eat first. You think it's stupid and eat when you are hungry. You don't help in the kitchen. Your house is like a hotel, it's like your all have a twenty four hour service going on. You look at how much work Indian cooking takes, and the pots that comes out of it. It puts you off. You hate cooking, because your father keeps telling you that you have to learn as if it's your job to learn, and Abhay keeps ordering you around. When you were thirteen, and got the pressure of learning how to cook, you fought with your mother. For her thirteen is half the age of a woman, and that's when your training to be a woman is supposed to start. All this doesn't make sense to you. You ask yourself, "Why should I go to school, if cooking and cleaning is so important in this culture." They drill it in your head so much that you just begin to hate it. You sometimes reach the point where you hate them all, and get tired of fighting with them. They don't seem to get the point, Abhay provokes you, knowing that your father knows how much you hate serving him and your brothers, your father still asks you to pour him tea. You have to leave what you're doing to serve him a cup of tea. You get so angry and say to yourself, "He has got a pair of hands and eyes, why can't he do it himself?" Still you do it for him. You are constantly arguing with the men in your house alone. Neither your mother nor your sister defends you. They look at you arguing with your father, your brothers and because no one else is arguing, the men in your house make you feel as if you are making a big deal out of it, instead of just doing it and being done with it. You get mad at them, Shalini and your mum. You tell Shalini and your mum, "It's because of you two that I have to go through this. You both make their beds, you both serve them and do what they tell you to do!" Your mother simply ignores you and because of that, your sister does it too. You are in a house with so many people yet feel alone. Abhay starts to call you a waste, and that's when you make it a big deal. It seems like the problem in the house is you. No one is complaining, only you. So many times you stand up for your mother and your sister, that you feel you waste your own energy for fighting for someone who doesn't fight for themselves, and when you need back up there's just no one around.

The boy who bullies everyone in class with his group of friends tries to make himself cooler by bullying others more. You hope he doesn't come for you, because you don't want to be embarrassed right now in front of Manav and his friend. You think, "Just imagine what will happen if these two tell my brother, Vivek will pick on me."

One Saturday you put so much chilli powder on your chips. Saturday night and Sunday morning your stomach hurts like mad. Your underwear feels wet so you go to the bathroom; you find blood coming out of you. You say, "Damn, I have got my period." You feel embarrassed; you say to yourself with all your heart, "I hate being a girl, why did I have to be one. Why didn't god make me a boy?" Your sister isn't there. You remember this being the subject of a girls talk between your friends and sister. She told you a thousand times what you have to do when you get your period, but it just sounds too technical for you. Your sister only got her period last year. Smita still didn't get hers. So many girls don't get period at this age that their mothers get scared and take them to doctors. You remember your sister being embarrassed when your mother took her to the doctor, on top of that he was male. You are embarrassed to tell your mother, you know what she is going to do, but say to yourself, "Give her a chance and maybe you'll be wrong." You go to her and say, "Mum, I have my period, what must I do?" She says, "Go in the room, sit there and wait for your sister." She follows you to the room, and you sit there and she closes the door. You say, "Right now I feel like I have a disease. Is it so difficult to tell me what to do? Is it so difficult?" You start crying, you promised yourself that the crying business is never going to happen, but right now you have the thought in your head that, "Why was I born, when this is the treatment you receive? Why did my parents even have me? Why did I come to this family, this culture? As far as this world is concerned, I don't remember ever asking to come here, and if I did in another world another time than it was definately the wrong choice. Why did I have to be this, a girl?" You stop crying, and tell yourself, "Wake up Saesha, wake up! It's not your fault that all this is happening to you! Don't waste your energy, your thoughts and your tears." You stop crying, yet today you feel very dirty and impure. You don't understand why you are feeling this way, just like the things that happened to you after the incident about Virsha's stepfather. Your sister comes after two hours and she tells you what do it. It's quick and simple, and you don't feel worse after putting the pad on, you feel better. It isn't a big deal after all. Your mother could have saved you all the grief and mourning process of your boy days being over. You tell yourself, "How lucky I am to not be a Tamil, just imagine having a ceremony for getting your period." In your group of friends, there is a Tamil girl. She told you that in the Tamil culture they have a big ceremony during the first days of the girls' period. She thinks it's embarrassing to make the first periods this big. She told you that it's that big that it feels like you're getting married or something.

Now it's difficult to get your eyes off Manav. Sometimes he is sitting near you; sometimes he is sitting somewhere in front of you, and sometimes he's sitting at the far end of the classroom. Sometimes you listen to the teacher and sometimes when it's easier and less obvious, you observe him. You know he's off limits, and you say to yourself, "Saesha, why doesn't it matter to you that he has got a girlfriend, why can't you stop yourself from looking at him, it's not like something is going to happen between you and him. He won't even like you back if he does find out. It's impossible."

In English literature, you wonder about him more. You have the same English teacher as last year. Somehow, the teacher teaches Shakespeare's work so passionately that you wish you could write that well. English literature inspires you. You're wondering to yourself, "I can't understand how this happened. I was sure; very sure, just damn sure that he wasn't my type." As days go by you observe him more, sitting a little close to him yet far back during one of the classes allows you to observe him. The way his hair sits, the way he holds his book, the way he writes; most of all, his pen, and the way he holds it. You write this down in your heart:

I wish that....,

that pen you're holding is me,
yet my love for you is in custody ...
you sit in front of me,
and can't even see...,
yet making it clear will not set me free...

You keep the secret with you for sometime. You see him with his girlfriend too, but they don't look that close together. One day, someone tells you casually,

"Manav broke up with his girlfriend." You are happy and then say to yourself, "For what should I be happy, when in fact it's worse. He needs time to get over her." You let some time pass and think it's time he should know. Smita, a girl in your group can't keep a secret. There's no way you can tell Manav directly, so you think of another way. You tell Smita, "Smita you know what, I like Manav." She's dying to spit it out, and you tell her, "Don't tell anyone." You know she won't be able to keep it in. The news goes around fast and he finds out first. When he finds out, he stares at you for a bit, you say, "Damn there's that overconfidence again," and get shy. It's like he's trying to get you to confirm it by looking at you, but you are too shy to look at him directly in his eyes, because your friends and his friends know and they watch both your reactions. Eventually the whole class finds out. Now the class just can't stop teasing you both. It's difficult to observe him like before. Now you have to hide and observe him.

You find out that Dean passed away. When you find out, you are shocked and it moves you completely. You didn't spend much time with Dean, his death and the way he died is affecting you. The fact that he is now dead, makes you remember the good things about him, during the time you all used to hang around together. You wonder, "Who knows he could have been my best friend once upon a time, the girlfriend he was dating until now could have been me. I could have been in so much pain today."

Dean was found in the park opposite Maxwell's house

where you all used to hang out once before. Maxwell tells you some member of a gang killed him. They didn't find the murderer. Dean was stabbed with a screwdriver, which pierced his heart. The killer wasn't looking to rob Dean. Maxwell said he had his gold ring and other valuable things still on him. It seems like the person who killed Dean knew him and wanted him dead. Dean was the only child of a divorced couple. You don't want to go to the funeral alone, and finally get the guts to do it. When you get to his house and see how many people there are, you tell your father, "It's ok, just drive pass his house." You can't get yourself to go in alone. His funeral is big. Your father says, "Going past also counts." You tell Shalini you couldn't do it because there were lots of people there. She laughs, "Hahahaha obviously there's going to be a lot people in a funeral." Not finding the murderer isn't a surprise to you. It's normal in your country. A lot of things are happening after the change in government. White people murdered, others being robbed, is just the beginning of what's to come. However, gangs have always existed in your town. Right now there are two big gangs that you really don't want to mess with. It's common to go to house parties, sometimes gangs show up, some of them have guns. If there aren't any gangs than there seem to be fights most of the time, and someone is always pulling out a gun. Normally when that starts, Jayesh says, "We are leaving. Now!" Seeing violence, is common, hearing about violence is common, it's part of daily life.

Juhi's knees often get swollen and hurt alot. This is happening a lot lately. Her father takes her to the doctors to find out what the problem is. The doctors tell her father that she has arthritis. She gets prescribed some medicines. You find out that she cannot eat the junk food you like. You avoid going there with your sweet and sour snacks. She asks you often, "Saesha you have any bor, or sour figs?" You say, "No Juhi, you can't eat them, that's why I don't bring them." She doesn't listen and makes you go to the shops with her, and sometimes sends you to the shops using her arthritis as an excuse. You don't want to buy her these things, but she doesn't listen. Now it's like you're becoming her slave, almost everything you once did together is changing, she makes you go and do certain things even when she's fine. You wonder to yourself, "I don't think it's good what she's doing. She's not exercising like the doctor said she should, and using her illness as an excuse can make her a slave of her illness for real one day." Chameli even tells her sometimes, "Juhi don't be lazy do it yourself." Juhi's grandfather tries to convince Juhi and Chameli's father to re-marry but their father doesn't want to so Juhi and Chameli's grandfather re-marries because he is worried about his grand daughters.

Lately you hang out a lot with a girl called Shilpa, Jayesh's close friend. You get along really well with her. You all go to her house and hang out sometimes. You don't know that Vinesh and Manav are in a football club together until someone says, "Vinesh found out that you like Manav while they were playing football together". You say to yourself, "Gosh what a way of finding out for Vinesh," but tell yourself, "It's ok, as it's a long time since Vinesh and I had last talked." Now that Manav knows, it's quite uncomfortable in class. He looks at you when you aren't looking at him and you at him when he isn't looking at you. It gets so frequent that you try not to be so obvious. Vivek finds out and starts teasing you, he acts so immature and by the way he teases you makes you feel uncomfortable and you deny it by saying, "I don't like him." Now Vivek and Manav are hanging out together, Manav is also hanging around with your brother's friends. He is sometimes in front of your house with the gang and you watch him from the window. You try to see his hair clearly, you observe his height, his body and say to yourself, "hmmm a sporty style, and he likes baseball type hats and the rugged jeans style. He is a sporty guy and I like the way he walks." You never observed these things in Vinesh, because you hardly saw him.

You cry sometimes about the incident that happened with Virsha's stepfather, but at least it's less than before. Falling in love takes over your life that Manav is in your mind a lot. It's funny how different this feeling is compared to liking Vinesh. Looking at Manav, thinking of him makes your heart beat faster. You're always bumping into him randomly. You change little things in your dressing and make sure you're always looking cool for bumping into him. You bump into him when you go to the shops to buy something, or when you leave the house for fresh air, or when you take a walk to visit Juhi and Chameli. He hangs out either at Ginas' Cafe, a five-minute walk from your house, or at his friend's house on your street. Eventually you see him so often that you know where he is going to be and at what time he is going to be there. You know he is falling in love the same way you are. Discovering this feels like you have wings and you feel like you're floating in the air. You never came to know this kind of love, and it's the first time in your life that you feel so good, that words aren't needed to tell you, to make you feel that this is the real feeling of love.

Things are changing, you don't have breasts, you are like an ironing board. You knew a long time ago that you should start looking out for yourself and don't confide in your mum and your mum hardly confides in you. Your sister only tells you what you need to know. You're not sure if it's time to wear a bra now. You watch the girls in your class, and almost every one of them is wearing a bra. You don't have breasts, and wearing the white shirt is part of your uniform that standing at a certain angle in the sun makes your shirt transparent. You also want to show Manav that you are an adult. You don't like the bra, so you opt for a sports bra. You've seen some girls wear it in class. You don't see the point in asking your mother, when in the end she'll go and tell Shalini to handle your business, so you go and ask Shalini one day, "I need a sports bra." She says, "I'll buy you one from where I work." Shalini often buys the latest fashion for Abhay and Vivek with her own salary.

You finally get your new sports bra. It's white, and it's very noticeable. You're not as obsessive as before about your dressing at school. Falling in love is helping you get over your incident with Virsha's stepfather. Love doesn't seem dirty to you anymore, it's something pure in your eyes. Your experience made you hate men and hate love. You still have times where you are uncomfortable with your brothers and father, but seem to be moving on from that incident finally. The more you fall in love the more stylish you become at school, trying to get Manav's attention more and more. Your changes are tiny, little by little and very subtle.

One day your father tells you, "Make sure you don't get taken for a ride." You know he is referring to your group of friends. You know what he means, "He is talking about sex." You laugh and say, "Was that supposed to be the sex talk that Indian parents give their kids. It's too late." One afternoon, you leave the house and head towards Juhi and Chameli's house. You see Manav walking in your direction, while you head in his direction. You have to pass him and get closer and closer. You really want to stare at him constantly, now and again you both look down, and finally you reach him and greet him, and just as you pass him you turn to watch him but little do you know that he'd do the same. Such small encounters with Manav makes your day complete, seeing him again, just one more time after school is enough to complete your day. You can't wait for the days in school where you'll coincide with him. At the weekends you also bump into him in parties and look forward too where you might end up every weekend, but when he's not around you don't enjoy yourself and can't wait to return home. The teasing in the class becomes too much that you both hide and find a way to look at each other. The bumping into each other is no more a coincidence, it's happening a lot. Your bag breaks and you even find a bag similar to his which you all write on. You walk in front of him when leaving class, turn to steal a look at him and find him staring at you as if he's seen something. Only later Smita tells you what she's done. Smita wrote, "Saesha

4 Manav, " and doesn't tell you until later. He comes in with a plaster on his hand one day, and the next day you have a bandage on your hand.

As much as you like your friends, something is starting to bother you. Whenever you go out, you ask your father for money and whenever you put in your part, you never receive your change. It's starting to become a habit and often Chameli says, "Pay with your fifty rands and we'll pay you back." Sometimes she'll take the full fifty and never returns the change. Sometimes she'll be short and say, "Saesha, I don't have enough, can you put in the rest for me?" You have to ask your dad all the time for money because they keep most of your change. Up to now, you lose right up to sums of thirty and sometimes forty rands in just one day. You try to take little amounts or change but you're always losing something by going out with them. Two rands here, five there, three there, and it's all adding up. When you ask for your money Chameli says, "She's crying for her money, give it to her!" It makes you feel bad. It then gets to the point that if Chameli isn't asking you for money, it's Juhi. You start to control the situation and say you have exact money. Now that you're falling in love you seem to have more confidence, you try and pick up more girl habits, and when Juhi and Chameli notice they bring it to your attention, it makes you uncomfortable so you go back to your old ways only when you're around them.

It's not enough to just bump into Manav, and look at him from far. Your heart desires more. You want to feel him, run your fingers through his hair, touch him, and kiss him. You don't know why he isn't making a move.

You wonder to yourself, "Why isn't he asking me out?" One day you hear a girl who is the sister of a boy in Vivek's group telling someone softly, "Saesha likes him for his money." This puts such a hole in your heart, it's only lately that you find out where his old house was, you still don't know where he lives. He's always coming from the direction you take to see Juhi and Chameli. You start to think, "Maybe all this is a game for him, maybe this is all I will have, nothing more. Look at your house Saesha, it's small, what does your family have. Maybe that girl is right, that's what Manav thinks." People tell you generally, "Manav is rich." You think to yourself, "What does money have to do with what I feel." Time goes on, and things stay the same between Manav and you. You start to think, "People are right, his money makes him better than me, maybe I'm just part of his game, I am not long term material for him." You hope you are wrong, and still have hope. You both still look at each other continuously in class. You try not to look at him for a few days, and he notices and looks at you more and more trying to make a point. You give up with your trial because you realize how much you love him. You say to yourself, "If doing this for a few days is so hard, what would it be like living a lifetime without him." Looking at him makes you happier than avoiding him.

You start to learn about the history of your country through English. In English Literature, you all use some set works written by South African writers. As time goes your eyes open. You didn't know that you lived under Apartheid until 1994. Apartheid is an Afrikaans word which literally means "separateness." Apartheid started in 1948 and that was the beginning of race laws. All races were classified and mix race marriages weren't allowed. A white could only be classified as a white depending on the way he spoke, his education, and manner. The best jobs, best education, best areas were given to white people. There were separate lines in post offices, and many other places for blacks and whites. There are four race classifications and they are Indians, Whites, Blacks and Coloureds; mixed race. All races were oppressed during apartheid but, Black people were oppressed the most while Apartheid favoured the white race. Some races, mainly the Black South Africans had to carry a book, which was often called the "dompass" by the Afrikaaners. "Dom" means "stupid or dumb" in Afrikaans. It had fingerprints, photo, address, name of employer, and more information about a person's identity. Some Indians also had to carry the passbook. People were put into tribal homelands, and the races were segregated. To access another area you needed your passbook to enter. The police patrolled around in a van called "Casspir," and if they found you without your pass in Johannesburg after a certain time, you'd end up in the "Casspir," and head to prison. Indians, coloureds and South African blacks lived in Sophiatown. They were then forced to move. Black South Africans were moved to Soweto. Indians moved to Lenasia, and Coloureds moved to Eldorado Park and the Chinese moved to central Johannesburg. Sophiatown was than re-zoned for white people. It was renamed Triomf, which means "Triumph." It turned out to be a suburb for poor white Afrikaaners. The Indians were put under a broader category; "Asians." In the Apartheid regime, Indians were also classified as blacks. You didn't know that you were living in this kind of a world until now.

Kalpana Masi always says that you all must come to America. Something inside you makes you want to go to America. You want to see Kalpana Masi. You think going on a holiday is possible, because last year Vivek went to India. Surely, it's not going to be a big deal. Now that you're older, you don't think that your father and mother will have problems like the last time you stayed over at Dharti Kaka's house. You are aware that it can be an expensive trip, and perhaps your father doesn't have that kind of money. So far, you haven't failed any exams and are doing well at school. You think your father will look at things that way. You decide to ask him. He is sitting and watching TV on the sofa. You sit down next to him and say, "Papa, can I speak to you?" He doesn't turn to face you. You repeat again with a louder voice, "Papa, can I talk to you?" He looks at you. You say, "Can I go on holiday to Kalpana Masi's house in America?" He thinks for a second. You say, "I'll understand if you don't have the money than I won't go." He says, "Ok, you can go." You think to yourself, "Wow how easy was that?" You can't believe it has been this easy, and make sure if you heard right. You say, "Papa are you sure? We have the money for me to go?" He doesn't answer. You ask again, "Can I go, you are sure about this right?" He says, "Yes." You ask your mum for Kalpana Masi's address. She gets Kalpana Masi's address for you from somebody. You write her a long polite letter a good few months in advance, a part of the letter goes as follows.

"I spoke to dad, and asked him if I can come for holidays in December to America. He said that I can

come but only if it's ok with you. I will understand if it's not possible."

After three weeks Kalpana Masi calls home. Your father answers the phone and speaks to her. He speaks to her happily. Your father then passes your mum the phone. You ask your dad excitingly, "Is she calling about the holiday to America?" Your father turns and looks at you seriously, he tells you angrily, "I was joking with you when I said you can go to America, why did you send her a letter?" You can't believe what you're hearing. You can't believe that this is coming from your father. It's your first time seeing this side of your father.

After the call ended, it's too late for you. You know that Kalpana Masi doesn't mind that you're coming for a holiday. You worked yourself up for the holiday a long time ago. You have your heart set on it. You can't believe he makes you feel like you made a big mistake. You don't expect this reaction from him, in fact you are surprised. You beat yourself up for this. It's hard for you to just turn it all around and say to your father, "it's ok I won't go." From the day, your father said yes, you had your dreams set on this trip. You decide to trade anything in your life right now for this trip. Before your father turns everything around, you approach him. You tell him, "Dad please send me to America, I don't have to go to College after high school, and you can use that money for this trip to America." You think that your father is not capable of leaving you without a higher education. When the time comes for you to study he will put in his part. It's the most important thing of all your life. Right now, you want to go to America, after all he told you from the beginning that you could go. He doesn't say a thing, and right now you are sick of receiving the silent treatment again. Eventually he decides to send you to America.

Abhay finds out about your trip. You think, "Isn't it funny that in this house, anything a boy wants to do is kept a secret and the girls only find out when it's happening or happened. Your father doesn't discuss anything with your mother and there aren't any family discussions. None of the women in this house come in their way, in their decisions, and your father's plans for them. Why is it that whatever a girl wants is always publicized and all the men in this house have to have a say? When are things in this house going to change?" You know that it cannot change unless your mother and your sister stand up with you.

Pravashni falls pregnant and is thinking of dropping out of school. You want to tell her to continue and not to give up but you aren't that close to her and don't want to make her feel that you are telling her what to do with her life. You take homework and the things she needs for her final exam to her house. You pray that she studies hard and passes, and with that, she will be able to see that she can do it. You believe she'll give up if she fails. Finally, she decides to continue but fails standard nine and has to repeat again. You are proud of Pravashni; she wants her high school certificate. You didn't think teenage pregnancies were a problem at school until it happened to Pravashni, and look at another example in your class. Some girls drop out of school so that they don't have to face the shame and very few of them have the guts to continue with their studies. In your school, it's common to get looks from people, or get called a slut or a bitch for being pregnant or being a mother at a young age.

You're closer to your friends than your own family. You hate being at home. Jayesh is more close to you than your own brothers. When your father finally allows you to go to America, you tell your friends. You are aware that they're going to ask you for a whole lot of things, you are also aware of the fact that they will not pay you back the money for the things they want. They give you a list of things to buy for them. It's a whole lot of expensive things. They guarantee you and say, "Saesha we'll pay you for all the things we want." You have heard that sentence a thousand times.

You pass your exams; and try a little harder this year. You don't want to give your father anymore problems. The ticket is expensive, and you feel really bad. During the planning of the trip, your father is happy. He isn't sure if he should give you more than one thousand dollars. You tell yourself, "Saesha accept the one thousand dollars; don't ask for more, it doesn't matter if you can't do a lot of things in America." Your father gives you two thousand dollars. You say to him, "I promise I'll bring back the change, I'll try not to use a lot." Abhay makes you feel bad for going to America. You say to yourself, "To hell with him, he did worse things to my father."

According to your itenerary, you have to change planes two times, once in Europe and once in America. Your father still looks happy; he doesn't seem as if he has a problem. Your mother's side of the family gives you a lot of things to give to Kalpana Masi and Anuj Kaka's family. Your family sends a lot of things for both Anuj Kaka and Kalpana Masi's family. You can't even fit half of your own things in with all the presents in your bag for both families, but think it's worth giving up some of your things because Kalpana Masi's family are worth it for their kindness in allowing you to stay with them. You can't wait to see Kalpana Masi and your cousins, you have good memories of her and them. You are amazed, and it's your first time on the plane. You want to be awake through the whole experience. Taking off and landing is exciting. The different buttons; even one for the air hostess, the free earphones, the way they serve the food, looking through the window; how high you are, and how tiny things look from this high, and the big, majestic plane. You stay awake all the way and make your last change in Detroit to catch the plane to Orlando, Florida. Unfortunately, you can't stay awake anymore and fall off to sleep on the last flight. It takes you two days to reach America.

You get to the airport, and can't wait to get out. You get your bag and get to the area, "nothing to declare" you see Kalpana Masi waiting for you. You get into her car and she's driving you home now. You are excited and uncomfortable at the same time. You don't know what to talk to her about. The area where Kalpana Masi stays is nice, her home is cozy. You are very shy. You have the habit of looking down while you walk and hardly look at people in their face when they talk to you. You don't observe things around you. You go around with your older cousin sister everywhere. You like her company and she is fun and outgoing. She drives and takes you with her on most occasions. She works in a part-time job in a restaurant in Disney world. Your aunty isn't allowing you to use the money your father gave you. You want to use it, and don't want her to pay for everything. You are aware that she is a single mum, looking after three kids alone. She wants you to get rid of your hip-hop style. You like your style, and she forces you to wear girlie stuff. You are uncomfortable in the things she's making you wear. You are not used to wearing colours; you only like your black and blue baggy clothes. Wearing red is eye catching for you, and wearing tights is so, so, tight that you feel stiff in them and walk like a robot. You look at your butt in the tights and want your baggy clothes badly. You are upset with Kalpana Masi and Anuj Kaka's wife for dressing you up like this, but it's just out of respect that you don't say anything. You miss home especially your mum, and say to yourself, "I want to be myself again. Thank god my mum isn't like them." You miss your mum and value her and the fact that she lets you be who you want to be. They give you a bag; you never have a bag on you. "Yuck who wants a bag," you wonder. In South Africa, having no bag is being smart. A bag catches the attention of thieves; you are likelier to be robbed with having a bag then going discreet. You normally separate your money in different pockets and are always prepared just in case you are robbed. Vivek got robbed this year, while he crossed the bridge coming from his College in Bramfontein to catch the taxi in Johannesburg. He was so angry that day. It's a common place for people to get robbed, but it's the only bridge that most students from College cross since it's close to the taxi rank.

At first, you are afraid of the White American people

and shy too, then later you find them normal and curious. Sometimes you get strange questions from the American people. The oddest one you got so far was, "Do you go to school on an elephant?" You have trouble understanding some American slang, that your cousins uses. Some of it you find funny, something that sounds like, "boogar" which your cousin uses when a seagull shits on him, and "rest room" which you think is a place to rest, and once you even ask your boy cousin if you can come in and see what the "rest room" looks like. The American accent becomes so contagious that even you end up speaking with an American Accent.

The holiday is going fine. Not communicating is a habit for you, and you don't know how to tell your aunty that she should take your money freely and use it for things that you are doing with them. You see your grandma. She's your mum's mother. You both don't talk much, you don't know what to talk about, she speaks to you in Gujarati, and you understand sometimes and sometimes not. Generally you answer her in English but if you can you answer in Gujarati. You both just sit together in silence after saying one line or one word to each other. Her favourite place to sit is in a very small room in the apartment. The room faces the garden. Anuj Kaka lives on the ground floor and the room where your granny sits has a roof and also has a fence from where you can see part of the garden. It's basically like an open room with a fence so you can see the green, green grass. Sitting there with your granny is nice, to hear and feel the air, and the wind. Somedays you both just sit there quietly looking at the grass, or listening to the rain and watching it drop onto the grass. You wonder what she must have lived through, or what she thinks about your mum's life or about you right now. Sometimes you get bored sitting with her, but sit there because you consider it as "The last visit." You know that it's not possible for you in this lifetime to return here and find your grandmother alive. She's old and you still have a long way to go, till you start earning money and to make this kind of money just to make a trip to America doesn't happen in a year. Your grandma lives with Anuj Kaka's family. You also have another uncle who was born with a mental disorder. Your mum sent toys for him.

Your grandma always wears a white sari just like your other grandma wears; your father's mother. In your culture when a woman's husband dies she must wear a white sari for the rest of her life. Widows are not supposed to look attractive according to your culture. The sindoor or red dot isn't worn. A sindoor is another way of showing your marriage status just above the forehead, where the hair parts. The same red powder that is used for making the red dot on a woman's forehead is used for the Sindoor. Your grandma doesn't wear any bangles, no jewellery at all. You are aware of such taboos in your culture, apparently the higher the caste the stronger the restrictions. Many years ago you understood that some women burnt themselves on their husbands pyre. This happened in some sub-culture community of Hinduism in India. Old black and white bollywood films had the act of the widow burning herself. The word for this is called "Sati." Sati means "faithful wife" in Sanskrit. It has something to do with the Hindu Mythology of a woman who burnt herself when her husband died. Sati is a voluntary act yet you also heard about the history where women were forced or expected to burn themselves by their inlaws because they were considered impure and also a burden. Britsh law banned this act in 1829.

You are not so close to Anuj Kaka, almost everyone you know doesn't like him. Kalpana Masi tells you one day that a fortune teller looked at Anuj Kaka's daughter Nutan's hand. She said something, which sounded like this in Gujarati, "Elok ne kidoo, ke Nutan doriyo hate nahi jahe." You are shocked, and repeat the words after your aunty saying, "Did a fortune teller really say that Nutan will run away with a white guy?" Your aunty says, "That's what he said, it was a fortune teller in India." From the day you arrived in America, you see life differently to yours. You realize why you need to make something of yourself, and say, "I will find a way to continue studying, this is a way to a better life than in South Africa." One day Kalpana Masi says, "You all should come and stay here, you, Vivek, Abhay, and Sita Masi's kids. We should do all your papers." This makes you happy. You say to yourself, "She's so nice, that if she helps me get here, I will help her so much."

You meet Kalpana Masi's best friend. Her name is Sapna. You call her Sapna Aunty. She's really beautiful, kind, and she helps Kalpana Masi a lot. Sapna Masi has long hair, and is a very intelligent woman. She is married to a muslim man. A lot of marriages between a Hindu and a Muslim aren't taken well by families and eloping is quite normal. In Sapna Aunty's time she eloped with the man she is with now. She has two kids, one daughter and a son.

One day Kalpana Masi looks at you angrily and asks you a question. You think you did something wrong when you see how angry she is. She demands an answer from you, "Who do you listen to more, your mum or your father?" You don't know which answer to choose, because in reality you hardly listen to both of them. Mostly in Indian families, the man takes the final decision, and you think perhaps the right answer to say here is Dad. Before you even answer, she accuses you of listening to your father. You try to think what you've done wrong. She says things to you that you really take to heart. Her words stab you right in the heart, and you feel the pain. She than asks, "Who bought the ticket for your trip to Orlando?" You lie and say, "Abhay and Dad paid for the ticket," since you don't know what's going on, you're not sure whether the truth or a lie will stop her from being angry at you. As you stand there your aunty gets a call, it's Sita Masi. None of your cousins are around. It becomes obvious that the conversation is about you and your family. Your cousins come onto the phone. Kalpana Masi greets them one by one. You can't believe your ears, Kalpana Masi repeats what each one has to say about you, your brothers and sister, "Aha, Saesha drinks alcohol and eats meat, even Abhay and Vivek." They attack each member one by one apart from your mother. You know some of these accusations aren't completely true. They had no right attacking Shalini. Shalini is the most obedient from all of you. They act as if they know everything about you and your family. You are frustrated and swear at them in your mind, "If you all don't know the truth why are you all barking here like dogs? What right do they have to judge me?" Nothing is making sense, you ask someone up there, "Why are they doing this god? Just why are they doing this to my family and me? Are they jealous of me being here?"

Now it all makes sense, your cousins didn't only come and pick you and your brother up for school in the mornings, but they were busy spying on the things you all do every morning to tell their mother. They got their conclusion from seeing you all eat eggs for breakfast. About you drinking alcohol, they make it seem like you drink glasses and glasses, when you can't even handle the taste of just one glass. Kalpana Masi's daughter drinks alcohol, when going out you both drank alcohol with her friends. You don't say anything, and keep that information to yourself.

You're starting to see the truth, and wonder and look back on certain events, you tell yourself, "Now it's clear. They were always in for smearing our names. They never say anything good about us, never. Now I understand why Sita Masi is always putting the pressure on us to buy a new fridge for the house, and keeps telling us what we need to do in our house." You remember not taking it well when she told you this, at the time you had your own problems to deal with. Sita Masi is worse with Shalini; she treats Shalini as if she's stupid.

Kalpana Masi tells you, "Don't tell them that you know all this, and that you were standing with me when you heard them saying these things about you." You think to yourself, "Of course I won't say anything, they mean nothing to me anymore. I will stick Sita Masi's daughter just this last coming year when she comes and picks me up for school. I will make sure that I won't

have anything to do with them when I finish school."
Kalpana Masi tells you, "Your father went to Sita
Masi's house and said so many dirty things about your
mother to Sita Masi's husband and her. Your father told
Sita Masi that he will give the house to Shalini and kick
you, your brothers and your mum out of the house."
You can't believe what you are hearing, this isn't the
father you know. You think to yourself, "This is all lies.
It's not true," you don't believe everything she tells you
because you never met this side of your father ever.
You know nothing about your mum's side of the
family. They always treat your all worse than your
father's side of the family. Kalpana Masi tells you,
"Your father bought a washing machine for his older
brother's wife instead of buying it for your mother!"
You confirm things to yourself, "Why should I believe
Kalpana Masi? I hardly know her. What do I have to do
with their past?" She put you through hell, and you
toughen up. To make up for everything that happened
she tells your cousin to take you out. You want to tell
your aunty that you want to get an early flight home,
but say, "No I won't let anyone win. I won't let my
father's money go to waste, this is what I wanted, I'm
not giving it up." You're not sure, if this is Kalpana
Masi's way to excuse herself from her ideas of trying to
help you. You do believe that your parents are capable
of making trouble. You so much older now, yet it feels
like the last time you stayed over at Dharti kaka's
house, so yeah you do believe part of Kalpana Masi's
story.

When visiting your Grandmother after that day nothing
is the same again. Things aren't the same as it was a
few weeks ago. Your confidence drops, you just don't

feel like being here and doing things with your cousins. You feel like a problem, and feel that perhaps they're embarrassed to hang out with you or something. You feel like a complete problem here. You don't discard the idea to return home earlier than planned and think it through. You don't want to make more work for your aunty. It feels like the past is repeating itself, Dharti Kaka's house, and soon your brothers and sister will throw all the blame on you.

You don't feel comfortable at Anuj Kaka's house, they act strange around you, whispering in the room and then come and talk to you as if everything is perfect, the whispering happens so often that you get the sensation that it's all revolved around you and your family. Sometimes it's just better to sit with your granny than to be around the people who are acting strange to you. You regret coming here and wonder, "Why did I come here? Why did I need to take this holiday?" One day Kalpana Masi tells you, "I am just one, and look how much I have and done, look what I've done for my kids, yet in your house with two parents your father can't even do what I've done. Look I've even bought my daughter a car." You are in her house, and it's making you angry but you stick it. She's going on as if you don't have any feelings. She's battering your father, and you wonder, "It's your father who paid for this trip, it's your father who is supporting you money wise up to now. America is a free country; it has more opportunities than South Africa. Anyone can make it here." You look at your aunty and think, "Well at least you have a rich friend to rely on, if things are difficult, my family relies on nobody." Kalpana Masi says, "Your all have too much pride."

Anuj Kaka makes you feel like you came here for free things. He tells you one day, "If you want to be rich than be around rich people." The tone he uses sounds like he is telling you, "To become rich, you should kiss rich peoples' ass", you're swearing at him in your mind, "I'm sure that's' what you do." You are not surprised with people's true colours anymore. You had some respect for Anuj Kaka, at least some but now everything is gone. Your beliefs are gone, all the good things you thought of the people you were close to are all lies. You think, "Life is a lie, people on this planet can't be trusted. Everything my life was built on, is gone, I don't even know who I am anymore." You have little need to buy your friends the things they want, your aunty controls your spending and pays for most things, she only allows you to buy presents for your family and few things for your friends, and makes sure you buy something for Sita Masi's family. "People are liars, life is a lie, people are fake, and this life is fake. If it's true what my father said about kicking me out of the house, than why did he bring me to this world, am I a mistake? There is no real future for me. He must hate me a lot to want to kick me out of the house. Why does he hate me?" You wonder and sometimes have this questioning look towards Kalpana Masi, "What do you know about your own kids, perhaps they're not telling you everything they do, yet you are busy giving me a lecture." You are thinking alot, and promise yourself that you will study and leave that place with or without help. You don't want to see any family apart from your own again.

One day Anuj Kaka takes you with him to the shops, you enter a clothing shop and he asks you to pick something. You don't want anything from him, you don't want free things. You say, "No I don't want anything." He still has the nerve to tell you, "I will only pay for it if it's a skirt!" Your mum's side won't let things be, it seems many on your mum's side of the family want to turn you against your dad. They don't seem to know anything about you, you love both your parents equally and would never choose a side. As far as you're concerned you never saw this side of your father and as far as they're concerned, they don't know the truth and just hear what is going on through other people. One day you feel completely used by Anuj Kaka, he makes you feel like he's taking you out but makes you watch a kid's film in the cinema with his children. You feel like you've been bought there to be a nanny. Kalpana Masi's kids say, "Anuj Kaka always takes other people who come here on holiday to Kennedy Space Centre, that way he doesn't have to pay for entrance hahaha."

Towards the end of your holiday, Kalpana Masi buys an almost one thousand dollar jacket for Abhay as a present from her. You wonder to yourself "Does he even deserve that?" You don't buy the things you want to buy for yourself, and can't wait to go home, you don't feel comfortable around here anymore. You want to go home badly, and that day finally arrives for you to catch the plane. You are extremely happy. Kalpana Masi tells you she's going to do your papers so that you can come to America. You are happy, because even though you had hell here, you know it would be different when you start studying and working. During the flight you think about many things. You are keen on becoming someone, and believe that you can, the fact that your aunty will help you with the main part; legalities will change everything. You are angry with you father for spoiling everything. When you land in Amsterdam you go and buy yourself a walkman worth three hundred dollars out of the one thousand that you are supposed to return with. You really don't care about your father's money and when you return you give him his seven hundred dollars. Your brothers are upset with you. They blame you because your father put less money into the house. They said, "We needed money and he won't give us anything." They tell you angrily, "Why did you insist on going to America when we don't have a lot of money?" and turn their back on your face and walk away. As far as you remember, you never insisted. They make you feel guilty and it's going on like this for days. Every time your father says, "NO" to them for something normal or something a little more than normal than it becomes your fault, all because you went to America. Your sister and your mother stand and watch the show; the problem in this house right now is you.

Dharti Kaka's daughter joined three other cousins on your father's side of the family to make a trip to India, while you were in America. It's not a surprise for you and your sister to be left out, after all what can your all do if you have problematic parents who don't know how to act like adults.

Your brothers and your sister don't know what your father did. Your father is making the whole family pay for the fact that you took a holiday to America. Now that you see what he is doing to your family, it answers your question clearly. With the way he is reacting, it's telling you that he did go to Sita Masi's house to make trouble. You keep it to yourself. You don't see your father in the same light as before and you are very disappointed in him. Your relationship with him changes. You feel very sorry for your mum but she and you are both powerless. If your mum ever has a best friend than it's Shalini.

Standard Ten

It's 1996, you need to think about your future, after America there are more reasons for you to become someone in your life, not only for you, but for your mother and your sister. America has opened your eyes about life. It's not impossible to realize things in America. When you return you want to become someone big in your life. Now Juhi has a boyfriend. Life in America is nothing like the life you are living here. You never bought the things your friends wanted and told them Kalpana Masi was controlling your spending. You did buy them some nice tops with America on it, but it obviously isn't what they wanted. They seem disappointed.

You return to school fifteen days late. Pravashni comes to see you and likes your American accent. For the first time in your life, like many Indians here, you all are shocked. You look down on the ground floor, and you blink to make sure that what you are looking at is actually true. You tell yourself, "White boy, it's a white boy...there's a white boy in our school." He is tall, blond, and of course he is really white. Everyone can spot him a mile away. As you all change classes you see "White boy." You and your friends are laughing at how everyone looks at him. Smita says laughing, "Everyone is staring at the "Doryo," this must be his strangest first day at school in his life." "Doryo" is another word for "White boy," Gujarati's use it among their own people to often refer to a White person. Well "White boy" doesn't seem to have a problem with making friends. Everyone is buzzing around him.

You have the same teacher for English this year too, and still learn more about apartheid. You had to see how America really is for yourself and that's because your country tried to keep people stupid by controlling international coverage. More and more you are moving into reality. You wonder about how many problems of your own you have that you never asked yourself about the political situation of your country. Things aren't the same with you and your father. The fact that it didn't only cost him money in sending you to America, it's going to cost him to make you leave this house. It cost you embarrasement and now it's costing his relationship with you. You still keep low, and watch him carefully.

Sita Masi and your cousins act like nothing happened. You have your eagle eye on them. Now you pick out the criticism in the way they speak with you all. You, your brothers and sister still treat them nice, and you never did stop to read the spaces in their lines. What has happened here is that they don't know what you know. You read the spaces in their lines clearly. You say to yourself, "I can't believe I've been so blind!" You give them their presents, observe their smile, and find them so fake. You think, "They don't even deserve the presents." It's burning you up inside to pretend when you seeing and living this war. Sita Masi starts again about the fridge, her kids make comments and you wonder about Sita Masi's comment and say to yourself, "It's not our fault that our mother is suffering, if you want to blame someone, blame yourselves for not helping her before things got this far, before we got this old." You ask yourself more questions, "Why does my mother's side never come to our house to visit us? What more happened with this family?" Sita Masi brought your cousins into a war that she should handle because your mother is her family, and the same with Kalpana Masi and Anuj Kaka. All your cousins hate your father and don't even know the real truth. They've caused a circle, what their parents are doing to your family, is now going to be done by their children onto you, your brothers and sister. Now you know why Abhay gets picked on by your other cousins on your mother's side of the family. You now see it clearly, they are making your all responsible for the way your mother's life turned out. You say angrily to yourself, "What, they need to find someone to blame, because they know that it should have been them, who could have helped my mother, all of us were just born in a middle of their war." You hate them thoroughly. Your own family are the untouchables when it comes to your mother's side, their kids know about a history, which they don't even know is true or not. Their kids are not even supposed to be in the middle of this. You think, "How stupid must my cousins be, to try and not attempt to find out the truth before knowing whose side to be on. How can they judge me and my siblings by the errors their parents and my parents have committed."

You are so tired of Manav and you not making your relationship concrete, that the constant bumping into each other, looking at each other, but hardly talking to each other seems endless. You wonder the same thing each time, "Why isn't he asking me to be his girlfriend? Why does he flirt around but never makes a move?" You have all these feelings inside you that can't be released, you take a paper and a pen and put down your feelings on paper.

"Is love supposed to set you free?
What is it doing with me?

Love is becoming tiring,
it doesn't get further than flirting.

Now I want to touch, taste and feel,
yet prefer being cursed into steel.

Why can't I just tell you what I feel?"

Now Manav is on your mind the whole day and the
whole night. You are tired of harbouring your feelings
and imaginations in your mind, if you can only just do
what you feel. You don't understand why Vivek is not
helping you, especially if he is close friends with him.
Your love runs so deep that sex before marriage doesn't
matter to you. This guy has become your life. You
wake up thinking of him, go to bed thinking of him,
your mind wants him, your heart wants him, and your
body wants him. In America, you wished there was
more between you both. You wish you had someone to
talk to. You know that your education comes first, and
learn to push him out of your mind.

You get your act together. You start to really look at
your life now and your future. "I don't have time to
play around. I have to make big decisions. Soon
Kalpana Masi will let me know about the process. I
need to know where I stand with Manav, and I need to
know now. I will give up America if he feels what I feel
for him. I'm going to have the guts to talk to him."

You go to Vivek for advice, and know that Manav is

going to confess his feelings to you. You are completely sure about it. You hope that Vivek will look at this maturely. You tell him, "Vivek I have to talk to Manav about something important." Vivek says, "He doesn't love you so don't go and talk to him! You're wasting your time!" You're not surprised with Vivek's answer. You know he will never help you and will stand up for his friends before his own sister. You tell Vivek, "Well I don't believe you, I would rather get it straight from the horse's mouth."

You ask Juhi's boyfriend to do you a favour. You tell him, "Can you call Manav and tell him to meet you outside his house tomorrow at half past ten at night?" Tell him you want to talk to him about something." You tell him "I made it this late at night so that none of his friends find out." Juhi's boyfriend agrees. You both plan it out well and Juhi's boyfriend comes and pick you up. You are nervous and already planned the conversation, but the problem is that what you planned and what might come out could end up being two different things. Juhi's boyfriend hoots in front of his house, and he looks out of his window and peeks his head out of the curtain. You are admiring the view. He obviously doesn't know that you all could see him clearly in his underwear. He changes and comes down, he definately didn't expect to find you waiting in a corner where no one in his family can see you.

Juhi's boyfriend disappears. Nothing can stop you tonight, you can count the times you've been this close to him. You want to kiss him so badly, and hope that he'll confess what he feels so that you can resolve this and move on to the next level. You are very nervous,

221

and worried about the rumours that will go around tomorrow. You can't look him in the eyes, even though you love them so much. You are kicking the sand softly with your foot and as you look down you tell him, "I want to do a lot of things in my life, and there's a big possibility of me going to America so I need to know where I stand with you." You want to tell him you love him, but aren't that brave, you say "I like you a lot. Do you feel the same way for me? That way I would know what I have to do." You already checked all your barriers and have the solution on whether to move on or continue with him or without him or even wait for him. You went through everything clearly even through possible answers he could give you. You usually prefer your answers in black and white, and expect just that. He says, "We can be friends." It catches you completely off guard. You can't believe you are wrong to think he felt the same. You definately didn't plan for that answer. You don't know what to think or say. You say to yourself after a few seconds, "Friends, what a stupid answer for someone who is definately in love with you." Your heart is broken and you don't believe that he doesn't feel anything for you. You accept his answer, and look at him clearly for the last time, your mind takes the last photographs of his face, his smile and you say goodbye to him and take a walk home. You know it's close to midnight, tomorrow you have to face him at school, and who knows what else you might face. You remember the looks, the coincidences, and say to yourself, "But Saesha how can you be wrong? This wrong?" When walking home, you realise that Vivek is right; it is just wishful thinking on your side. Your heart is weeping, "It's a year now that you both have been flirting, and it's all just in your stupid head

222

Saesha." You actually believe that there is something truly wrong with you. You are battering yourself, "How can I see something that is really not there? I am such a fool! I'm the dumbest person on earth." You convince yourself that you were stupid to think that there was any chemistry between you both. You don't sleep well that night, it drives you mad and nothing adds up, to think that you were wrong about certain events and certain reactions of Manav. You say to yourself, "I went there to get an answer right? I got it, so why hurt myself more? I will forget him for once and for all!" You are nervous to go to school the next day. Since last night, you have been strengthening yourself to forget about him, and to keep your feelings to yourself. You promise yourself that you are going to stop looking at him, bumping into him, and flirting with him. You convince yourself on the way to school and come to the conclusion that you are wasting your time with this person and that it's better for you to concentrate on your studies and future.

In class, you are a group of four friends. The four of you talk about the incident that took place last night. Juhi is laughing because her boyfriend told her that he saw Manav in a black jockey. The girls laughed so loud. Smita often acted immature. She is very traditional, and likes to sing bollywood songs. When Manav comes to school, you don't act the way you did before. He has the habit of looking at you. You notice him coming into class, but don't look at him. In fact the whole day you do this. School is boring now, but mostly it's hurting you. Manav's friends find out that you went to speak to him, you wonder if he told them the truth. You feel him staring at you, as if he's waiting for you to look at him back. You wonder if he's changed his mind over what he said to you. Three days gone and it is starting to hurt you, Manav still keeps looking at you like before, and you don't return the looks, and give no signs. Juhi is hitting your leg under the desk to tell you that Manav is looking at you. You feel like he's treating you like a toy, this isn't friendship. Smita gives Manav a name, "black jocks." Malar the fourth girl in your group is laughing one way. Smita is a typical conservative Indian girl who jokes around a lot. You all can never talk to her about sex on a serious level without her laughing all the way through the conversation. In the end, you can't handle not looking at Manav. You are happier looking at him and it gives your heart a kind of happiness and satisfaction. The fact that it works two ways still makes you happy.

Your boy cousin's wife gets a baby girl and your father's mother past away. You and other cousins have to choose the name for your cousin's baby. In the Hindu culture, the priest chooses a Sanskrit letter for naming the baby depending on the date and time born. Normally when a brother has a child, the sister does the child naming. In the case of your cousin, he has no sisters. The Sanskrit letter is "VA" among other letters. You already know what name to choose for the girl. You, your sister and Dharti Kaka's daughters are there. They all say it's difficult to find a name with "VA." As far as you and your sister are concerned, that's the day they're going to name the child. You say, "I have a name." While Dharti Kaka's daughters are shouting out various names you shout out "Virsha," the name of the only best friend you had in your life. Someone says, "Saesha, nice name!" You wonder if the parents of the little girl heard your option. They tell your family when to return. When you return, Darti Kaka's daughter acts like the name you chose came from her. It seems like the parents of the girl who you all were bought to name, give the credit to Dharti Kaka's daughter. There's no point opening your mouth for this after all they are closer to Dharti Kaka's family. Shalini tells you, "Saesha you picked that name, it's your best friend's name." You don't care anymore.

One day Sita Masi tells your mother, "Tell Saesha not to hang around with Pravashni, she might fall pregnant too." You are just tired of so many people coming into your house and telling you all what to do. It's always been like this. You just think all your family are full of it, there is not one family or cousin who you really can say is true to your all. Your brothers are men, what do they know when everything is in their favour. They can't even see what women go through in this family. You wish you were already working, perhaps then you'd be more independant and can make the choice of not attending any family events.

One day Smita says, "I don't want to be at school today." You all say, "We too." You all plan to stand by the gate during breaktime. The gate's still closed but it isn't locked, there's your chance. You already had four classes. You are all planning to dodge school today but Smita is more desperate at getting out today. The bell rings and break time is over. As you all hide behind a fence with some plants. You see one of the school's worst teachers taking his students to the field. This teacher is the worst in the sense that he is just very strict. He is the Physical Education teacher. When you

225

all see the teacher, you all say to Smita, "Ah na! Let's call it off, look at him, just imagine what he'll do if he catches us?" You all peep from above the fence to see if he's occupied and quickly duck. Smita turns to face you all. You think it's possible to get away with it, but you also think that you all are four, and just how are you four going to slide through the gate without him noticing. Smita tries to convince you all, but you all aren't very convinced. She says, "Ok watch how I do it and come." You all scream "No! Don't! We're not following you." Off she goes and she actually manages it, but now you all can see her, through the plants. You all say, "Why isn't she running?" She screams with a low voice, "Come on, what you all waiting for?" Instead of running, she waits for you all. You all don't plan to move from there. You see two students running in the direction of the gate and realize that they're behind Smita. Smita makes a runner, and the boys are chasing her. You, Juhi and your other friend get out of there and back into the class where you all belong. You all are hoping that Smita made it out.

At least twenty five minutes past, and Smita arrives into the class. You, Juhi and your other friend see grass all over her long, black hair. She comes and sits in her place. You all ask her, "Smita what happened?" She says, "Why didn't you all just come?" She says, "Well the boys were chasing me, I ran so fast, jumped into the garden of one house, when I saw that I lost one guy, I tried running into another house, and saw a big dog, it went "Wow, wow," so I tried finding another house, and jumped that wall too. I struggled to jump that wall but I made it. I didn't open the gate it looked locked, but the guy didn't jump the wall, he just opened the

226

gate and pulled me out from where I was hiding. You all say, "So you jumped the wall instead of opening the gate?" She laughs and says, "Yes." You all dust the grass off her hair, and are surprised that she's still laughing about it. You expect her to be angry with you. Mr Khan your english teacher puts you all in groups to perform a play out of a section of Macbeth. You have the freedom to choose the part you want to play. You and your three friends are deciding on the part, but you already know which part you want to act out. You want to play out the drunken porter. You convince your friends straight and they like the idea since it will be funny.

One Friday you stand on the white fence in front of the patio of your home to see if Manav is by his friends' house, or if he's heading in your direction. You decide to stick around there for a while so he can see you from far. When he sees you, he usually comes in your direction as an excuse to hang around at Gina's Cafe. You try to balance yourself on the fence and while trying that you miss a step and land with your legs between the fence and hit your groin, chin and face on the bar. "Ouch!" you scream. You try to recover really quickly and try to get out of the embarrassing situation and look around to see if any neighbours are outside or if someone is looking through their windows. While trying to recover from your embarrassing position you hit your face on the bar again. As soon as you got out of the situation, you run into the house and go straight to the mirror. You have a dark red line under your chin. You sigh with relief, because it doesn't look that bad, which means you don't have to go to school looking strange, especially with Manav around. As the hours pass, marks appear on your face. You stay at home for two days finding ways to hide the marks, which went from red to black, you also find two black marks on both sides between your nose and eyes. You try to find everything possible to cover it up but nothing works. The make-up base you find is light for your skin tone.

It's Monday morning, and you try the make-up base even if it doesn't work. You are about to make it through the whole day without any questions. Your last two subjects for the day are English, a double English class. Today you are all going to do Literature. All the girls in the class like Mr Khan, the English teacher's ass. Mr Khan gives his class and often jokes around in class. He askes you a question about the subject you are all learning about. Normally if you don't know the answer than you'd have this blank look on your face. He glares at you for a moment and says, "What are those marks between your eyes?" The whole class directs their heads towards you, your three friends who are sitting in a line next to you also turn to face you, they are all staring and waiting for an answer. You think, "Shit!" Now Manav has a good reason to look at you for longer than usual. You look at him and the rest of the class and then turn your head to face the teacher and say, "I bumped into a pole!" Manav is the first one to crash into laughter and seconds later the rest of the class starts to laugh. Now you are in the second half of your Literature class and Mr Khan says, "I need to leave the class for a short while." The class gets noisy and your three friends are still laughing about the answer you've given the teacher. Smita says, "What kind of a pole did you bump into?" I mean we all know it's not true, the kind of pole you must have bumped into must have been square." You know she's right, there aren't any square poles in your town. You tell them in short what happened, and they laugh so hard. You say to yourself, "Now having these marks in class makes things more comfortable at school, after all I bumped into a pole, right?"

Sita Masi calls your house, and wants to speak to you. She tells you, "Kalpana Masi spoke to your father about opening a file for you to come to America. Your father said no. Kalpana Masi has got three kids, and has to do a lot herself." You get the point, and you ask yourself if the conversation even took place between Kalpana Masi and your father. You don't get it, "Why would Kalpana Masi tell you all these years that you and your cousins must all come to America." Right now, it's really easy for both sides to lie, after all Kalpana Masi made you aware about your father in America. Sita Masi and your cousins managed to smear your name, so why would your aunty want you around. Your father never communicates with you, he doesn't care about your future, and even if he is a complete fool, he'll never tell you what he has done to your mother, and most of all he won't even see that he was wrong. You say to yourself, "Fair enough, it looks like I'm on my own. Only they know what's the truth."

You come to Juhi and Chameli's house, and the maid opens the door. You go to the room and find Juhi speaking with her boyfriend. It seems as if he wants to break off with her. She threatens him by telling him that she'll kill herself if he breaks up with her. Chameli and Jayesh don't like Juhi's boyfriend that much, and Juhi is very secretive with them about her relationship. You can't believe that Juhi is using these tactics to force him to stay with her. You and your three friends now practice your parts for the play.

Shalini now works full time in Delta Spar. You weren't convinced from the beginning about her studies. You ask yourself, "What is she doing with her life?" You approach her and tell her that she must take on some serious studies. She gets angry with you when you tell her she must study something good. She tells you, "You think life is easy, real life isn't as easy as you think." You wonder to yourself, "Studying something else isn't difficult, because your father doesn't mind paying for her." You feel like you're wasting your time, she thinks you're a kid and doesn't even listen to you. She is trying to learn how to drive, and instead of choosing a driving school, which is recognized, she picks a school that doesn't convince you. You say, "Here we go again." Your father offers her all the money in the world for her studies and licence. Your father still gives you, your brothers and sister money for going out. When Vivek needs to shop for clothes he asks your father, and they go shopping together. When you need to shop, you need to find your own way to buy things yourself. He doesn't give you enough. You don't see him giving your mother money. You wonder, "When is the last time she bought something for herself? Shalini buys her what she needs." If you need tampons, your sister buys it for you.

It's time to do the play. You know this will make Manav and the class laugh. This is your way to impress Manav. The teacher points to your group and says, "Ok now it's their turn." You are ready. You have your shoes off, two different coloured socks and one with your toe sticking out. In one hand you have a bottle of Bells, inside there's water instead of scotch whisky, and in the other hand a huge, black dustbin bag. You get up, and the class is already laughing at you. You place the dustbin bag on the floor in front of the class, and get in. The whole class is laughing. Everyone positions themselves for the play.

Macbeth, Act 2 Scene 3

Malar – *Macduff: Was it so late, friend, ere you went to bed, That you do lie so late?*

Saesha – *Porter* (coming out of the plastic bag, drinking bells, getting up drunk and with a drunken voice and acting like a complete drunk) *Faith sir, we were carousing till the second cock; and drink, sir, is a great provoker of three things.*

Macduff: What three things does drink especially provoke?

Porter: Marry, sir, ...painting, ..., and urine...., sir, it provokes, and unprovokes; it provokes the desire, but it takes away the performance. (*Macduff, Lennox*-Smita, and *Macbeth*-Juhi are looking at each other, you seem to forget some parts) ....; *makes him stand to, and not stand to; in conclusion, equivocates* .... (the class is laughing one way)

Porter confuses *Macduff, Lennox*, and *Macbeth, Porter* skips *Macduff* for some reason and continues with the play.

That it did, sir, (class laughs even louder) *i' the very throat on me; but I re- quited him for his lie;......, yet I made a shift to cast him..*

You all eventually pull it off, and the fact that you forgot you parts worked out well since it was the part of drunken porter.

You are trying to get your learners. You wrote the learners a few times and you're still failing. Saesha tells you that she did hers orally and it's the fastest way to get it. You do it orally and get your learners. Shalini is going to this driving school forever and he still keeps telling her she is not ready, she even tells you it's like he isn't interested. You know the man is ripping her off. You tell her, "Why do you keep choosing the worst ways to get to what you want?" As far as you're concerned, the fashion-designing course was really a waste and didn't last too long. It didn't even look professional. You think to yourself "At the end look where she ended up, in Delta Spar and now the worst is that she doesn't even want to study." Finally, you have reason with this driving school, only you don't tell her, "I told you so." You start taking a few lessons with a recognized teacher. The same teacher Vivek had for his lessons and licence. You hear she's very good. You take one lesson or sometimes two a week. The lessons are expensive and your father gives you money to learn how to drive.

It's been a while since Juhi and her boyfriend ended their relationship. You know that if Juhi doesn't get her act together she's going to end up alone. Her boyfriend paid for everything, and bought her expensive clothes.

She expects him to pay everywhere they go. She never pulls out money for anything. One day you walk in and find her with another guy. You know the guy, he is the friend of the guy Virsha dated when she ran away from home. He is surprised to see you. You talk to him for a bit, but leave after a while. You can see he is very interested in Juhi. As you walk home, you wonder about him. You hope and pray that Virsha didn't tell the whole world that her stepfather molested you. As you walk home, Manav's cousin hoots and asks you for a lift. You are grateful, yet say, "No thanks." The next day, Juhi talks to you about it, and then Chameli and Jayesh finds out. Jayesh is really upset. He wants to kill the man who did that to you. You say, "It doesn't matter, I'm over it now. It's not worth it."

It's getting closer to the end of the year. You start to concentrate on your studies knowing that you and Manav are going to be separated by the end of this year. You both have to choose a career after high school. Things in your life get more unstable and you know you could end up anywhere or couldn't end up studying what you want to and consider the fact that it's highly possible that you won't be able to study where you want. The biggest question of all is, "What exactly do I want to do with my life?" The fights at home get bigger between you and your father. Your father and you don't talk about your higher education. He normally brings up the subject with your brothers and sister, but doesn't even ask you about your higher education. You think, "This probably means I have to fight for it."

You don't know what options you have. You want to go to the University. A University where almost everyone in this town goes to because it's recognized internationally as well. You know that the University is expensive. You go to the open day and find a course which you want to study. It's a degree; and you don't have many choices because you didn't take up maths and science. You think it's worth studying this long to have a good qualification. You find a course but the price of these courses are around the same. You don't know how much your father makes in a year, your brothers know more than you. You have all your information ready to approach your father.

One evening, you go to your father. He is watching television. You use a logical way than the one you used to go to America. You know that you've traded your studies for America, but hope that he won't leave you without an education. You say, "Papa I have to decide about my future and what I want to study." He doesn't answer you. You need to put in an application soon and need to get the reply before the beginning of next year. You say to your father, again, "If you don't have money to send me to University I will study anything, but if it's possible than I need to do my application now." You hand him the paper with the prices. Since he doesn't know, you explain to him. After explaining to him you tell him, "Think about it and then we'll talk about it another day, and if we don't have the money, than I'll find something else to study." In a few days Abhay comes to you and tells you sarcastically, "So you want to go to University, why do you want to go to University? A paper means nothing, going to work and getting experience is worth more than a paper." You say, "It's none of your business what I want to do." Abhay shouts at you and says, "What a waste, when are you going to get it through your head that we don't have that much money for you to go to University!" You don't even know whether he is drunk or sober, all you know is that he made his choices for his own life, and money for his studies were never an issue. It's only now that your father doesn't support him a lot, and that's because he just messed up so much.

Now you approach your father for the answer to your question. You are desperate and need to study. He's watching TV again and it's really irritating that you have to start the conversation. You say, "Papa did you think about it?" He doesn't answer you. You don't think it's a difficult question, and think to yourself, "I mean he must know the kind of money he has. It can't be so difficult to answer whether you have the money for me to go to University or not." He doesn't answer, he stares at the television. He sends Vivek to College and gives him everything he wants and keeps telling Shalini that if she wants to study something he'll pay for it. It frustrates you because you know he has money. You say, "Papa if you don't have that amount of money for University how much can you afford?" He ignores you and looks at the TV. You don't have patience for this and with an angry voice you say, "Tell me something. If I have to pay you back for studying than I'll do it." He raises his voice and tells you, "Didn't you say to me that you didn't need to study, and that the money for your studies can be used to go to America." You can't believe it, it makes you angry that you are paying for his mistakes. He had a choice the day you asked him if you could go to America and he made that choice. Now you are really angry because you feel that you were never in his plans. It makes you angry that he

235

doesn't care about you or your life. You ask yourself again, "Why the hell was I born if I have no future here, and you never planned one for me." You both get into an argument, and he shouts, "Get out of my house!" You can't believe it, your father is kicking you out of the house because you want to go to University. The argument isn't even big enough to get kicked out of the house. You think, "Other parents are proud that their kids want to go to University, and you're busy kicking me out." You leave, and you are so angry, you don't want to return home again. You walk out of your house, you bang the white gate, and get to the second gate, and bang that gate too. You want to cry, and you are angry, but you see Manav heading in your direction. You don't look at him, you look down on the ground and walk very fast. You are very angry. Everything is just a fight in your life right now. You wait for him to pass and don't turn around like you always do and after some distance you start crying. You don't know where to go and don't ever want to return home again. Tears are running out of your eyes even though you try and keep them in. You are walking so fast that they get smeared by the air and spread all over your face. When you see people on the street you look down. Your sister heard the row, and all your mother does is sleep. Tears are just running, and you can't let it all out, you just want to sit down and cry somewhere but there's no where you can do it, only at the park in front of Juhi, and Chameli's house. It's around nine O'clock at night. You head to the park, and sit on the swing and cry. You go to Juhi and Chameli's house, because you see their lights on. Juhi opens the door and you tell her, "Can you come and sit with me in the park. She sees that something is wrong and tells her sister before she comes out." Eventually Jayesh and Chameli comes too. You tell them what happened, and Jayesh is shocked. He can't believe that your father kicked you out for something like this. Jayesh says, "How can your father do something like this and if it means I have to pay for your studies I'll do it." You know it's all words. There's no place you can stay tonight, your friends can only help you so much. You walk back home, they all have to go. Out of pride you don't want to go home, and you get home, ask Shalini for Abhay's new car keys. She gives it to you and you go and sleep in the car. You think about Manav's life, and realise that you both are cut from different material. His life is sorted and yours is hell. You can't pretend living like him, you have to grow up, now you have to do things for yourself. You say to yourself, "I don't have time to play Manav's games; after all he has a normal family." You think about Kalpana Masi's words, and you remember her telling you, "Your grandfather bought this house for your mother and your father paid him back." You wonder, "At the end of the day, my father is a useless man." You hate your father like never before. You know that all this could be prevented, getting kicked out of the house was not necessary if he just gave you a simple "Yes" or "No", or even a simple explanation just so you know what to do with your life next. When Abhay returns he asks Shalini, "Where's Saesha?" Shalini says, "She's sleeping in your car, Papa kicked her out of the house." Abhay gets you out of the car and says, "Go inside, come on, inside." You shout, "I don't want to go into his damn house, if he wants me out, I'll sleep in your car. He can stick his house up his ass." Abhay looks at you sympathetically and says, "Go inside, come on. Don't worry about him." It's as if he's

237

been here before and knows the feeling.

Now it gets hard to avoid someone you love when he's in your class, when he is your brother's friend, when he comes to your home sometimes, when you leave the house he's walking past, or just when you think you won't see him, he's further down the road by his friend's house. Juhi's grandma, the woman who her grandfather married blames you for Juhi's arthritis. You don't think it's fair. You tell Juhi a million times to stop eating that stuff, it's not your fault if she's buying it on her own. One day as you, Juhi, Chameli, and Jayesh are driving to a place, you talk about your studies, because you worry about it. Chameli says, "Not again, Jayesh can you just tell her to stop with this subject of her studies." You didn't know that it was bothering her all this time and keep quiet. Jayesh says, "Chameli, you should understand, it's really important when it comes to making a decision this big about your future."

You make your application into University just in case. You say, "If life wants me there, than it will happen, and by putting in my application I won't feel a sense of regret for my life." You get rejected for entry into University. You wonder, "Everything is so unfair for me, why is everyone's life around me is so easy? Why must I fight for everything?" After apartheid, affirmative action was created and only if you have money you can bribe someone to accept your entrance. After Apartheid, universities accept a high amount of Black, and Coloured South Africans, but a low amount of Indian, and White South Africans. Now all Indians are complaining that they are not too black for the system and are always in the middle. You resent affirmative action, and you all practically call it reverse apartheid. It's giving opportunities to the races affected during apartheid, but it doesn't look at how rich or poor you are to study something. You say to yourself, "What have I got to do with this country's past, and just all of the sudden I'm just supposed to pay for something that I didn't know existed, something that someone else created in the past. I am just starting out in this life." Your father finally tells you, "I'll pay for your studies. I only have ten thousand rands for your studies. That's my last responsibility to you." Vivek is fighting to study again, he is so upset. He even tells you, "Because you spent the money to go to America, I can't study." Your father still has the seven hundred dollars you brought back from America; he doesn't mention that to anyone. You think to yourself, "Well if we don't have any money for our education, than it must be a lie. Why would he keep the seven hundred dollars, which is seventy percent of the College fees." Your father puts another ten grand for his studies. You wonder, "How fair has this world been so far. I didn't fail, not one year in English school, and because my brothers and sister failed, the costs add up just when it comes to my turn. If they just did the job to pass when they had to, I could have actually studied what I wanted. Now my father has to pay for my studies and Vivek's at the same time."

Your father wants to resign his job. He want to go away to India for a few months. You know after this it's over, you won't receive anymore money from him. He is getting difficult. You have ten grand and your brother is studying what you like. Just for the sake of studying, you study something you don't even like. You don't want to be two in the family studying the same thing, and you end up choosing "Hotel Operations and Management." You don't even know why you chose it, when you hate being in the kitchen, and hate cooking. It's the Matric ball, a party for all people who finish high school. You decide to get a really nice dress to impress Manav. A dressmaker from Pakistan makes it for you. It costs alot. You want him to remember you and this day. He always wears a blue cap, and so you pick the colour blue for the dress. You are looking forward to seeing him in a nice suit. The classes who are a year below yours helps organise the Matric ball and are also invited to the ball. Pravashni is there with her boyfriend. Smita is the only one missing from you four. You see Manav and he's dressed no where close to what you've imagined. At the ball, you all find out that Pravashni gets beaten up by her boyfriend. The older guy in your class who lightly bullys you all sometimes, sees Pravashni's boyfriend put his hand around her neck, walks with her in a direction where there aren't many people, he makes a fist with his hand and hits Pravashni's face. To your surprise, the bully in your class stands up for her, and almost gets himself in a fight with Pravashni's boyfriend. You only see the part where Pravashni's boyfriend drops his fist after hitting her and you tell her to stay away from him, but when her boyfriend finds out about what you said, Pravashni and you hardly see each other.

One day you walk into the middle of a question. Your mum's asking your brother, "You drink?" Abhay is wondering what's going on. She says, "Devi Masi's son saw you drinking in a bar." Abhay says, "Aha, yes, I was drinking beer in a bar, and Devi Masi's son was drinking tequila with his wife. They probably thought I

240

was going to spy them out, but it looks like they wanted to smear my name first." You are wondering, "Is Devi Masi so stupid to not ask herself what her own son is doing in a bar?"

Now the rape rate in your country is growing rapidly. You come to accept that if things are meant to happen than they will happen. You don't have much control over the situation. You think to yourself, "If ever I get raped I will kill myself, I can't live through that." You worry about Shalini too and start liking guns. Abhay has a nine millimetre. You think it's in your interest to get one too. Shalini's dressing isn't changing, she dresses so bad that you wonder if she's doing it to put men off. You hope she's never been in a similar or worse situation like yours.

You have to wait for your Matric results. It will only come out during the holidays in the newspaper. Sita Masi's son tells you, "I'll look for your name in the newspaper. You are expecting a Standard grade pass or Matric Excemption?" You say, "Matric Exemption." Sita Masi's son says, "If you get a Matric Exemption I'll call you." You wonder to yourself, "Why do you even need to call?" He tells you, " I will call you to congratulate you." You think it's a really nice gesture, but know that he doesn't expect you to get a Matric Exemption. There is always something new with your mother's side of the family. If it's not that you doing something wrong, it's about school, once you put them straight there, they're always finding a new problem.

During this year, you drink a glass of wine now and again, not too often, because you still aren't use to it.

You stopped eating meat a long time ago, after Virsha moved away. You used to eat once in three months with Virsha and thought you don't need to have it after she moved away. Besides, you can live without it, you are not used to its taste and it makes you feel guilty for eating the animal.

You almost started to eat meat again. After what Sita Masi did in America because you thought, "Why be good, when they made it seem like I eat loads of meat, and drink loads of alcohol. I stopped eating meat a long time ago. What now just because I eat egg, they say I am eating meat. It doesn't serve to be who I am, it doesn't serve being good when it will mean nothing, people just want to smear mine and my family's name in this society." People don't allow you to show them the truth, they stain and keep your name stained by your past. Luckily, you come to your senses and think about it for a while. You made a personal decision then and say, "I believe in doing the right thing for me, if I feel it's right than it should only matter to me. The world can say what they want about me, it's only me who knows the truth."

One of Jayesh's friend takes their son to the paediatrician because he has a bad flu. The paediatrician gives him the wrong medication. Their son dies in your private local hospital. Jayesh is really upset. His friends took their son to the paediatrician because he had a bad flu, but the paediatrician gave him the wrong medication, and because of that, their son died. Before the death of Jayesh's friends son there was an incident at the same hospital. A person had to remove their appendix but didn't have ten thousand rands up front to pay for it, the person ended up dying at the hospital. No justice was ever served to the parents who lost their child. Public hospitals don't have enough doctors and waiting forever is normal. You either pay for medical care or die.

You need extra money to do certain things this holiday. You wonder if you have to fight again for money for driving lessons. Your father gives you some money for driving lessons, but at times it's tough, and you ask Shalini. You will be eighteen soon, and plan to do your driving test after turning eighteen. You want to put this behind you, driving lessons are really expensive. Shalini did her driving test and failed. She has spent a lot of money in driving lessons. Jayesh has a friend who charges a little bit of money for driving lessons. He isn't a certified driving teacher but knows how to teach and what to teach for the exam. Shalini needs to practise more, and you give her the telephone number of Jayesh's friend.

Juhi breaks off with the guy who was friends with Virsha's ex-boyfriend. He was cheating on her. Juhi and Chameli are making a trip to India this year with their father. You don't ask them for anything. You remember what it was like when you went to America. You're organised with your studies, and are prepared for next year. You remember saying to yourself the last time you left Delta Spar, "My days of being a sales lady are gone." As much as I hate the job, I could do with some money right now. You ask Shalini if Delta Spar is looking for some full time staff for this vacation. She finds out for you, and before you know it, you start to work there these holidays. When Chameli and Juhi leave for India, they ask Jayesh to look after their cousin's house. Jayesh says, "Saesha and I will hang out, and she can help me with things." You don't think that you'll actually end up hanging around with Jayesh, because it's uncomfortable, and besides he's just saying that because you're standing here. He is Chameli's boyfriend. Now working in Delta Spar is harder than before. You see a girl working there, she used to be with you in MDDActive. You are happy to see her. You don't work where Shalini works, you work on the floor. It's the worst job and you have to be on your feet all day. You're not allowed to sit. You have to help customers, carry their baskets, and take it to the till. If you sell a lot, you get a commission. The girl who you meet from MDDActive always tells you that she has some good music and that she'll bring some so that you can record it. When you see her again she hands you a cassette. You say, "I'll listen to it, and if I like it I'll record it. I might take time in returning the cassette to you." She says, "Sure, why don't you listen to it now. Tell your sister to play it." You say, "Good idea, ok."

The radio is behind the counter where Shalini works. Virsha and Mitali use to blast the same radio. You don't think it's a problem, because others bring their own music sometimes and put it on. Delta Spar is more relaxed than you once knew it to be. You hand the cassette to Shalini. Shalini says, "No, No, this radio is for here, the radio for the music on the floor is over there." Shalini is pointing to where you have to go. You go to the corner where Shalini's pointing. You ask a young guy who you speak to now and again, "Would you mind playing this cassette for me?" He says, "Ok, no problem." The music starts to play, you don't hear much because it's noisy, and sometimes you are busy talking to the customers. Now and again, there are songs that you recognise. You are working hard. Your customer finished paying Shalini. Just than you, hear Tikku Bhai's deep, serious voice on the mike, "Saesha to the office." Shalini is about to laugh, she knows how scared you are of him. Your face changes from a nice fresh, red, shiny, happy cherry in the summer to a scared, shaky, fragile, dried leave in the winter. You wonder to yourself, "What did I do now?" You march up to his office thinking, "I didn't do anything wrong, don't tell me he is going to tell me that he is going to cut my wages. Not again after all these years!" You try to walk bravely and don't want to show him that you're weak, you think to yourself, "Who knows he might be looking at me from his office right now."

He asks you, "Is this your cassette?" You are wondering, "What the hell is he talking about?" He says angrily, "Listen!" and before you even get a chance to answer him. He repeats again, "Listen to the song."

"Cuz I will be a freak until the day...until the dawn, and we can (pump, pump), all through the night till the early morn...
Come on and I will take you around the hood...on a ganster lean,
and we can (pump, pump) anytime of the day, it's all good for me... (It's all...)"

"Now you listen to music like this!" shouts Tikku Bhai. You are more scared of him shouting then answering. You didn't find anything dirty in the song, until it came to "pump, pump," and kinda made you say inside, "Oh!

no!" You didn't know the cassette had this kind of music. You don't want to get the other girl involved. He says, "Take your cassette out and don't bring this kind of music again!"

You leave his office and as you leave his office, you pay attention to the next song,

" oh, oh, oh... You got me humpin day and night, oh baby... oh..."

You are running and screaming in your mind,
"Oh, oh, oh,
I gotta stop this cassette,
before he makes a big show..."

You go to the guy and say to him, "Can you please remove the cassette?" He says, "Sure," and goes away for a moment, he returns and hands it to you. You eventually tell him to return the cassette to the girl who borrowed it to you. She works in that corner too.

On your way home you tell Shalini the story, and she is laughing sick. You say, "Why does he always do this to me and nobody else?" You are a little embarrassed to work at Delta Spar. You don't want Manav to see you, and think that you plan to be a big nothing in your life. You hate the Delta Spar van, and it's really embarrassing. You pray, "I hope Vivek is not standing with Manav anywhere near our house when I come home."

.22

You slide in the ammunition one by one, really quickly, round end facing the opening of the magazine, push down on the opening of the magazine, and slide it in with your thumb, ... done. You pull back the slide. Now quickly you press the Mag release, and catch the Magazine in your hand with your other hand, put it onto the table, pull back the slide, a bullet comes flying out and then check the barrel. "Saesha, you're going too fast." You say, "Ok, I'll slow down." "Ok now do the whole procedure, don't remove the ammunition, pull back the slide and prepare for shooting... but slowly."

You slide in the bullet into the Mag, the bullet which was in the barrel that came flying out, you push the Mag into the slot, and press the slide release and safety on. "Very good, Saesha." You say, "Shall I shoot?" He says, "Of course, what are you waiting for?" Your gun is at a ninety-degree angle, safety off, your one foot is forward and the other is back, aim and fire. You don't hit your target point on the board. When you finish you unload the gun for Shalini.

You are losing fear for the gun since starting a few weeks ago. Shalini and you go on Sundays to practice at an outdoor shooting range. While you are doing your training today some people are watching. They've been watching you through the whole procedure. Shalini is doing her training, so you look at them directly. Someone in the group says loudly, "Vinesh it's Saesha." You still have your hip-hop style going, you think, "It's kinda cool doing this." Vinesh and his group have guns too, but they have a designated area for paint

247

ball.

The gun makes you feel powerful, and cool. Now you can relate to how guys feel when someone messes with them. Watching Abhay with his gun is interesting, the way he cleans it and handles it. You are dealing with a little gun here, while Abhay has a nine millimetre. You plan to get your gun licence and then a firearm. The rape rate in South Africa is on the increase and if the incident with Virsha's stepfather was so difficult to handle, you can't imagine how being raped must feel.

You and Shalini, go to gun lessons together. You both will get a certificate for it. With the firearms instructor, you both learn how many accidents have occured and keep occuring in your town. "Boy sees father putting the gun away, dies." Guns stored with the barrel loaded and accidents occurs, kids taking guns to school, thinking they're toys injures other kids, Cop kills himself and family, teenagers wanting to get revenge on bullies, and so many gun related accidents and suicides. Hindu, Muslim, Christian, and coloured races, it's all the same, different headlines yet similar stories.

Now there's so many things happening in your town. A little girl from the primary school where you went to gets raped in the field near to the school on her way home, a university student gets kidnapped, she was being watched and everyday was at the same place and same time waiting for a bus. You pray it's not you and your sister next.

During the holidays, you hang out with Jayesh at times. When he decides to go to the cinema, you want to say no, but quickly he tells you, "Juhi's cousin is coming with us too." You are always saved. There's no way you will like Jayesh, he is just not your type. You are too in love with Manav. You sometimes go to Jayesh's house and talk to his older sister. His older sister insinuates a lot. She doesn't seem to like Chameli. Just to make conversation you ask her, "Did Chameli call to say hi?" She says, "Yes, she called the night you and Jayesh went to the cinema." You say quickly, "No, her cousin also came with us." She says, "Yes I know, I just told Chameli that you went with Jayesh to the cinema." You know what she's doing, it's like she's trying to make Chameli feel insecure. You say to yourself, "Chameli is not stupid, her relationship with Jayesh is really strong, she won't see it the way Jayesh's sister is making it look like." You don't think anything of it, and think it's nothing big.

You have your heart set on avoiding Manav, you tell yourself all the time, "I just want to forget him. I JUST WANT TO FORGET HIM." You see him when you really don't want to. You make it clear to him by giving him an angry look. It's your way of telling him, "I don't want to have anything to do with you." One day you decide to go to Gina's Café. You decide to go there at an odd time so you don't bump into Manav. As you enter the entrance of the shop you hear...

You gotta really breathe her, really taste her
Till you can feel her in your blood ...

"Hello," you say to Manav. "Hello, can I have this and this please," you ask the shop keeper.

You know you really love a woman.

When you love a woman,

"Thanks, bye" you tell the shop keeper, "Bye," you say to Manav. You are walking out the shop

Tell her that she's really wanted,
When you love a woman tell her that she's the one.

On the 2nd January 1997, Shalini and you get your basic firearm certificate. You sigh and say, "I still have a long way to go till I get my gun." Juhi and Chameli return from India. You miss them a lot, but the best eye opener this holiday is that you see how much money you're saving by going out with people who don't rob you. You don't even want to think about how much they managed to get out of you. That thought just makes you angry.

You finish working at Delta spar, and now you say for sure, "Now I don't ever want to come back to being a sales lady again. This is definately the last time I'll do this job."

One day, as you relax and sit in the area of the garage where Vivek used to have his English classes. You look at your mother's plants. You turn away, and quickly turn back to look closely, "Is that what I think it is?" you ask yourself. You go closer, and move the plants with your foot, they don't move, you push with a little more force, and find that it rolls a bit. "It's my skateboard, that's where it was all this time, mum hid it from me, and put her plants on them." The board is worn out, and looks fragile after being there, through years and through different weather conditions.

Reality

You see Juhi and Chameli very little, it's strange but then you figure that they are pretty busy. Juhi's maybe planning for College and probably they're busy settling down after coming back from India. The last time you bump into Juhi, she asks you where you are going to study? You tell her the name of the business college where you will be studying. Juhi isn't sure what she wants to study as yet. A girl invites you to her party. She's in Chameli's class, and you speak to her now and again. Her cousin likes Vivek a lot. Juhi, Chameli and Jayesh are also invited. It's strange that they didn't mention anything about the party. You don't know whether you are all going or not. You aren't going to go alone if Juhi, Jayesh and Chameli don't come along. You call them to find out if they going to go to the party. Chameli exclaims, "We'll meet you there!" She doesn't tell you a time, or anything. You find all this strange, because coming to pick you up is on their way to the venue. You think, "Ah! It's not a big deal, I can take a walk, it's not far from here anyway." You get dressed and decide to go late, that way you'll be sure that they are there.

You see them and greet them. You hang around with them like always; you finally turn around and see them in the other end of the hall. You walk up to them and hang around with them until you turn and don't see them there. You look for them and can't find them, so you go and stand near a stage by the front entrance so that they can spot you. They see you, and Chameli has a look on her face, it's as if she hates you. They don't approach you, they stand their ground. People are looking at you, you feel like a disease. Everyone notices what's going on, and you are embarrassed. Almost everyone in the party knows that you four stick together like glue, and this is why it catches their attention. You think to yourself, "What am I doing here? Why are they doing this? Why did they choose today to do this, in front of everyone? Why can't they just tell me what the problem is, aren't we supposed to be friends?" It hurts more to stab someone this way, with this many people looking; it hurts so much that leaving will hurt you less. You say to yourself, "I obviously mean nothing to them; we are obviously not the friends I thought we were." You feel deceived, and you say to yourself, "If that's the way it's going to be, than that's how it's going to be." You are sad to say goodbye to this friendship and walk away sadly, but than the birthday girl comes in front of you with her group and starts dancing with you. You dance with her a little bit, and when they seem a little occupied, you walk out the door, without turning back. You tell yourself, "If they want my friendship back they are not going to get it back easily." While you walk home, you try to add up how and what happened here. It's clear that they don't want your friendship anymore.

You are on your own now. No friends, no boyfriend, no money. You think, "Jayesh is supposed to be older and wiser. He just turned out to be the the same age as Chameli and Juhi by allowing them and himself to do things this way." You never felt this kind of a stabbing feeling inside you by the way they've done it, "I don't want to go through something like this again. Why am I not good enough for them suddenly?" you wonder. Shalini gives you some money to pay for the driving lessons you have now and again when your father doesn't give you money. You are close to the end and soon you will take your driving test. Shalini is taking a few lessons with Jayesh's friend.

Everything is really demotivating for you right now. You sit down and think about your life. You feel like your role on earth is to be a fool. "Just think about it," you tell yourself, "Why don't you have a boyfriend? Why don't you have friends? Why don't you have anything in this life the way you want it?" You really do feel like a fool today, and tell yourself, "Look, Juhi is set; she already has transport to go to College, her father works in Johannesburg. Manav, well he doesn't have the problems I have. It's obvious I mean ... What do I have to do to show that I'm just as good as them? Nothing, absolutely nothing. It's over, it's over, this time it really is. It's time to make a real life, and live in this real world."

You have to start College now, you don't even know how you are going to get there everyday. Juhi doesn't need you, her father goes to Johannesburg everyday, so she has a lift to go to College. No one advises you. You tell yourself, "It's fine I'll find a way on my own." Vivek catches the taxi to go to College. At least you have someone to walk with to the taxi rank every morning. On the first day of College, you both have to get up really early to bath, and walk thirty minutes in the morning before catching the taxi. It's really depressing for you. On your first day you say, "I hope Manav doesn't see me." Unfortunately on the second day while walking to the taxi rank you think he sees you." Vivek waves at a car, which hoots at him.

Every morning Vivek and you catch the taxi into Johannesburg, and then from there you both walk to Braamfontein where you study. You tell yourself, "If it wasn't for Vivek I wouldn't have had the courage to go to College by taxi." Stepping into these taxis makes you uncomfortable. You feel more like lower class shit. All the people you know find a lift club. Lift clubs are formed by a group of people from the same town going in the same direction, sometimes one of them has a car, or various people in the group have a car and each one just pays their part of the petrol.

You don't know many people and many people don't want to know you. While you and Vivek walk to the taxis, some people in the cars always hoot at him on the daily basis and while Vivek waves, you look for the car that Manav is in. Manav is also in a lift club; he goes with a guy whose father was a teacher at your high school. The teacher died last year, but before he died, he won some money and with that money, he bought a Mercedes for his son. Manav travels with that group to University. Every morning you are looking out for the car that Manav goes in. Even though you just see him for a moment, and knowing that he sees you brings the magic back, it's just too strong. You learn to accept this situation; walking to the taxi rank everyday, and come to the conclusion, "If people can't accept me for who I am, than it's too bad. If this is what I have to do for my future than it will be done. If this is how real life is, and it's just the beginning, then imagine what else will be coming my way." Somedays it's freezing cold especially if the taxi you and Vivek are in doesn't have heating. Coming home on your own using the taxi makes you nervous. When the taxi is coming closer to your stop you have to scream out loud "Stop!", or something short so that the driver can pull over. If you don't scream loud enough he continues. This has already happened a few times only because you were too shy to scream. One day Abhay sees you cramped up in a taxi, while he sat in a car with his boss to go to work. He comes home that evening and brings you down. In fact he is embarrassed that the people including him who rode to work with their boss saw you sitting in a cramped taxi.

You miss your friends, and you miss going out. You are now permanently at home on the weekends. You look on the bright side of life, and tell yourself, "Saesha, at least you are proud of who you are, even if you have nothing. It's time to forget what everyone thinks of you. This is what you have, this is what you are." As of now you get used to thinking this way and realise that it's actually a blessing to have no friends. You have lived your life by their opinions, their desires; never did you end up doing what you wanted to, with them. You always went with their choices. The friendship was one way. Juhi and Chameli bought you down when they saw you changing for the better. You think to yourself, "Well at least I can be myself now without getting stressed."

You see Juhi at College, yet have the courtesy to say "Hello" and "Goodbye" to her, nothing more and nothing less. She hardly has any friends, and neither do you, yet you prefer it this way for you, you won't ever forget the day they've cast you out in front of everyone, you know that feeling very well, just taking you back to that day, is enough to make you keep your word about keeping your distance from them.

You turn eighteen and in a few days you have your first driving exam. Your father pays for the exam. You really want to get your driving licence on the first time. You don't know anyone who got it on the first time so far everyone you know failed on their first test. You are nervous, your driving teacher sees the person who is going to test you. She tells you, "If you have four hundred rands, he'll accept it, he'll pass you if you pay him." You can't believe your ears. It was your first exam and you want to do it yourself. You tell her, "No, I'll try and do it myself." You do well, and come to the parallel parking, you hit the "fake pole" and you fail the driving test. Your father is really difficult to get money from, and so you don't ask for more money from your father to take more lessons or to try and do the exam again. You really want to but things are really difficult when it comes to money.

The Poet

Now that you don't have many friends, and have a lot of time to think. You wonder, "I actually miss Literature, and Shakespeare." You say, "I wish I could write as good as Shakespeare. I wish one day I'll be one of the greatest writers that existed. " You are really motivated to write like him, reading your old English Literature books, makes you want to write. You make a pact with yourself, and decide to train daily at writing poetry. A lot of it comes with natural inspiration.

Day One

"Love

Is love an inspiration by one or by two?
To some it's a connotation!
To some the feeling is new.
Many are blinded by its charm,
and are left numbed.
Love can be left undone,
by some who either have another one.
Love cannot always be fun,
you always on the run.
Hope is what you may lose,
yet you still can't refuse.
You are forced to let go,
yet to let go is to be free,
and to come back is to keep.
Don't let your mistakes reap,
but let love reel,
and let love seep.
Let it go further than a reef,

into distant lands,
with love in both hands.
But be-aware my friends!

In memory of just how love hurts!"

Day 2

"This time I wish...?

I wish that this pen that I'm holding is you.
I know when you love someone it's for true,
Yet I know in my mind that these words are so few...
and may not change anything between me and you.
You probably should have been this paper, so I can
throw you away,
or tear you in two.

I can't bring this to an end...
Soo... I'm leaving it in your hands.
I definately don't want us to be friends,
and want to have a relationship and tie all the ends.

Love is no more this early morning dew,
and if whats in me now, was to be in you,
It would be a torture to you.
Soo... just crush me, or tear me in two!
Or cherish me as I cherish you."

Not all poems come with inspiration. You write, and make an effort to make it good, as a step to become a good writer. You make an effort using the thesaurus, yet hate reading books, but love reading sonnets, and poems, it's a hobby for you. A poem for you is like a

259

picture or a painting, it has rich colour, which you have to look deep inside to see, feel, touch, and taste. You have to capture its essence and look for the figures of speech. It's an art. Lately all you write is about love, and tell yourself, "A real writer needs to write about everything." You try and write about the night, the weather, the stars, and a lot more.

When you return from College, you see the daughter of the Muslim family. She was in your class right up to the end of high school. You both got along well at school. Her name is Lamiah. Lamiah has strict parents. She speaks to you, when you're on your way home from returning from College. You spend hours talking, and sometimes it's in your interest to continue talking when you see Manav standing right in front of her house. Now that you have a fixed schedule, you know when you'll see Manav.

It's 13:00pm, a hot, sunny day. You are returning from College. You know there's a ninety percent chance that you'll see Manav. Manav is a drug for you, you see him when you most desire, and keep wanting to see him more and more even though he is deadly for you. You feel free these days, no controlling friends. You are now used to taking a taxi, and can even do it on your own. You just miss Juhi, Jayesh and Chameli when you feel like going out.

You are changing a lot, your style, your ways, and looking back, you realize that you are completely over about what had happened with Virsha's stepfather. Falling in love changed everything in you and about you. You now go to College alone. Vivek is on practicals. You stand and talk to Lamiah one day and Manav is standing right in front of her house with his friends. Juhi, Chameli and Jayesh pull up in front of them, Manav and his friends look in your direction to look at your expression just as they pull over. You don't greet them and they don't greet you. People are wondering why you don't hang out together anymore, while some people's expression just tells you what information they've been fed. You even think that it changes Manav's feelings towards you.

"Rejection was something I was scared of then.
That's why I can't talk to you again.
So get your act together,
for I won't be there forever.
Friends can help you with opinions,
and it may serve your decisions,
but you'll never get to see,
unless you judge or know from within."

You are surprised to find that Manav is still interested in you. Everything is still normal between you. You see Jayeshs' sister one day. She comes and talks to you. Jayesh's sister mentions that she goes to work in the same direction as you when you go to college. She asks, "If you want to join me, I have space in my car. I will charge you, but it won't be expensive." You tell her how much you pay when going by taxi, and she works out a price for you. You don't want to get into any other issues with her and plan to talk about other things. She knows that something happened between you, Juhi, Chameli and Jayesh. Many days pass since you start travelling with her. She says, "I would have asked Juhi to join us but she won't pay for the transport." You know that Jayesh's sister doesn't like Chameli. She mentions the time when Chameli called, while they were in India, and tells you what she told her on the phone. You don't care, because as far as you're concerned, you are better off without them, even if someone tried making problems between you all. Life has done you a favour.

You have some nice and fun classmates in your Hotel operations and management course and class isn't that boring. You enjoy going to College as it's much more fun than High School. Sometimes you get bored during some lectures and write poems.

"The boring lecture

All the stupid theories,
Maslows bloody theory...
Early in the morning,
we already started yawning,
how boring.
That same old tone,
Ann feels all alone,
while I'm thinking of my phone."

You are worried about Shalini's future. She is now a sales lady. She changes jobs and finds a really nice place to work. She works in a white area and gets a better pay. She has transport to work there, and it's pretty decent. On Saturdays, her employers buy her lunch. She works for some Muslim people. You have grown up a lot, that you often wonder how. It's like magic. You were so short; the second shortest in class once upon a time, and now you are tall. Your breasts are a little bigger than before.

Meanwhile South Africa's violence and rape rate is growing even more. The reasons for most of the rapes are because of a lot of Sangomas. Sangomas' are traditional doctors in the Zulu culture and are also called "Witch Doctors." A Sangoma is an African medicine man and even practices witchcraft. Some Sangomas make money using stupid people. They tell a rapist or someone with AIDs that they would need to have sex with a virgin to be cured from AIDS, which was linked with a myth. Now there are many child rapes, even babies are raped. South Africas population is growing with AIDS victims. The news gets more and more shocking each time and now it's not only about HIV, family relatives including some fathers are raping their kids, gang rapes on women and babies. The most shocking news for you right now, just took place two days ago right in your own town. Two African women were walking through a field, when a group of men surrounded them. They were brutally raped, and as one of the woman laid there on the ground a man from the gang took a bottle, which lay nearby, broke it and pushed the neck of the bottle up the woman's vagina. She died and you wonder. "It doesn't matter if it was of internal wounds, she was probably dead inside after being raped brutally, any woman would be dead inside after that. What is the government doing? Why aren't these people caught? Why aren't they in prison?" Assaults, rapes, are now coming to the high school you once studied in. Robberies near your home, break-ins, thieves with guns, enter people's home. You can be raped, get beaten or tied. Some robbers enter houses wearing a police uniform. No matter how much protection your house might have, they still get in. These days people even get shot with their own firearm. A teenager in Durban dies for not handing over her shoes. It's come to a point where Blacks are raping blacks, killing and harming even their own kind.

These days you see one of your neighbours a lot. She comes to your house to get some poems. She likes your poems and you don't mind giving her some of the things you wrote. She wants mainly the ones on love. You meet Shilpa one day, she's not friends with Jayesh anymore. She tells you she's getting married and invites you to her wedding. You tell her you'll come. At college, you make friends with a girl in your class who is from Pietermaritzburg. Her name is Janese. She is short, has brown skin, and nice curly black hair. She is cool, and you have some good laughs together. You call her "J". J and you hang around a lot, she stays with her grandma in your town. The same thirty minutes you used to walk once to see Virsha. On Sundays you both decide to hang out and play pool. You go and pick her up by her house, and find that Janese's grandma is neighbours with Dean's mother. You say to Janese, "You knew Dean?" She says, "Yes, he was so cute, all the girls died for him. I pity how he died." You go to Janese's grandma's house often to hang out, and one day as you come out of Janese's grandma's house you see Dean's mother. You never met her before. Janese and you get into a conversation with her. Dean's mother tells you Dean's birthday is coming up soon. You tell her, "I knew Dean; I use to hang around with him and Maxwell. My friend was going out with Maxwell. Maxwell told me what happened, he even said that whoever did it, hasn't been found yet." Dean's mother, says, "I think Maxwell was involved, I went to his house and confronted him when all of this was going on." You are shocked because Maxwell was Dean's best friend. Nothing adds up, you think that Dean's mother is crazy, she is still very angry and is still in her own way, out there looking for the killer. You conclude, "That's how a mother can get if justice hasn't been served." Dean's mother gives you and Janese a printed picture of Dean to remember him. You walk home thinking about what Maxwell told you about that night Dean was killed. He mentioned it was foggy, and Dean usually walked alone to the park when coming to Maxwell's house. You remember him doing that during the day and night. You wonder, "Just how can Maxwell be involved?" You feel sorry for Maxwell, as far as Maxwell goes, he was a nice person, and he was no way capable of killing or plotting a kill on his best friend. He too lost his best friend, Dean's mother and Maxwell had the same loss. You think, "Just how much stress can it be to have the mother of your best friend blaming you for her son's death." You think, "Saesha maybe Maxwell isn't the same Maxwell you knew when he dated Virsha, maybe he's changed." You look at Dean's picture and you wonder for a bit. You pull out a pen and paper.

"They say that when one dies young,
they become an Angel,
but in this life exist devils.
Stabbing, hitting, firearms,
death can't be out run or undone.

I forget the day in April,
Your mother talks about how you were delivered.

I remember you being so calm,
And could never cause any harm.

What a terrible ordeal it has been,
dying alone in that scene.

It's something you didn't deserve,
and just where's the justice that should have been
served?

You were known to everyone,
and won't be forgotten by anyone.

"In memory of Dean."

The poems just keep coming and you can't stop it. You write poems about the fun moments at College, you write passionately about love, summer, nature, and about an infinite number of things. It now comes to you naturally.

You are doing well in the Hotel operations course, even though you don't like it a lot. You get distinctions in so many subjects. You are surprised to even get those kind of marks, you have never seen distinctions in quite a long time. You enjoy the wine tasting course. You are all served a five year old wine, and a ten year old wine. You are not going to just swirl your glass and whirl the wine around in your mouth, spit it out, and take a sip of water... you say, "No way. I am going to swallow it. I am not going to let such a good wine go to waste." It's a little difficult to continue the wine tasting afterwards, while everyone says different fragrances of each wine yours is completely off. At one point, everyone smells an apple fragrance while you smell a peach fragrance. That day you cross the main road in green and all the cars go passing you. You are still, in shock, until a few cars stop to let you pass. You also have Mampoer tasting a few days after the wine tasting course. It's the Afrikaans word for Moonshine. It's named after Mampuru an African chief. Mampoer is a home-distilled "brandy" made from fermented fruit, made from different fruits. It has a very high level of alcohol. One of the fruits used to make Mampoer is Marulas. Marula is a tree that grows in Africa. It's a wild fruit. The fruit is green, and when ripe it is yellowish in colour. The Marula can grow very high and the fruit is also used to make a popular liquor called Amarula in South Africa. Elephants enjoy eating the fruit of the Marula tree. While doing the Mampoer tasting you find out that they have a high alcohol content, many have over fifty percent alochol content. After you all finish your Hotel operations and management course, Janese will return back to Pietermaritzburg, the others to their own plans. You all exchange numbers and hope to meet up again. You all won't see each other until Graduation, and right now you all have to do practicles.

Abhay sometimes comes home drunk and irritates you all. Your father is making it difficult for you to get money out of him, he won't give you anything. The worst thing is that you need the money for important things. You say to yourself, "If it's like this now, what's going to happen next year?" You are close to finishing your studies and now you are busy doing practicals. You love working in the bar, making shots and cocktails are fun. The barman shows you how to juggle bottles when the manager isn't around. You hope to get a job at the place where you do your practicals. Unfortunately, they aren't hiring. You finish your studies in Hotel operations and everyone at home except your sister and your mother starts pressuring you to find a job. Vivek is working at a travel agency, the travel agency where your dad bought your ticket for America. The pressure is too strong, and you open the yellow pages to look for hotels and start calling to look for a job. Your brothers and your father start to complain about the phone bill, and every month it becomes a big deal. You are desperate to get a job, you don't want to be in this house anymore, it's just too much sometimes. One day you accidentally bump into a briefcase that Vivek has. You open it and find all sorts of information in it and some things on travelling and working. You find details for South Africans to work in United Kingdom, and the requirements needed to qualify for that. One of the requirements are that you have to have twenty thousand Rands in your account. You are only seventeen years old, jobless, inexperienced, and facing affirmative action.

Your house is too small for the amount of people it has in it. None of you have your personal space. You eat alone most of the time. You want to leave this house so badly. One day a fight breaks out between Vivek and Abhay. Your father watches them instead of separating them. Both of them are throwing fists at each other. It is clear that you all aren't even a real family. You wonder, "This is the last thing my house needs right now, a fight between two brothers, to show just how unhappy we really are in this prison we all call "home." The one who starts most of the fights usually, is Abhay. He provokes everyone. You wonder, "Abhay is supposed to be older, but what should I expect from a brother who goes on like this all his life?" You stand there screaming and try to stop them from beating the hell out of each other. Vivek does his things quietly and Abhay just comes from no where picking on everyone, telling them what he wants to. You can't understand what his problem is, the way you see it, "He had his chance to live differently and chose wrong. Everyone had high expectations of him, he had all the money to make something good out of himself. The only waste that you can see in this house right now is him. He doesn't let anyone live in peace."

It takes a while for Abhay and Vivek to get back on talking terms again. Another fight breaks out, and you don't know what the argument is about now. You argue when you think Abhay doesn't make sense. Abhay tells you, "What do you know? You were still small. We all had to go outside the house, when your father wanted to give your mother a hiding, and we all tried to look through the front window to see what was going on." You remember one day, you actually remember one day you were watching your brothers and sister looking through the window, from the outside yard, but you were too short to see anything, and wondered what they were looking at. You never knew that your father was abusive to your mother until now, now the pieces are starting to add up. You hate your father, yet you have to depend on him. That really does annoy you.

You don't see many friends around, many disappear little by little ever since you stop hanging around Chameli and her clan. They don't come looking for you. You see the difference between not having friends now too, when you hung around with Chameli, Jayesh and Juhi you used to be cool because you hung around with them, but now you're not cool anymore. For others you are no competition to them now, someone with nothing and therefore they don't want to be around you. Others don't even greet you anymore when you see them on the street.

As for you the fights and arguments in the house are endless and getting kicked out is now normal. Your father doesn't give you even a cent. You walk out and come back late and often think in your walks, "If I had the choice to run away forever and had money, I'll do it right now, in this moment, I won't even need to think about it. I don't want to see my father's and brother's faces again." You don't get along with anyone, everyone has their own war here. The more pressure they give you, the more you look for jobs outside of your city. You look for jobs in the coast, Cape Town, and Durban. You want to be at the coast, far, far away from home. As the days go by some things just get clearer for you, "Manav and I have different lives, different obstacles, my fight is greater than his. I am not some rich girl, I can't wait for him. I just can't wait for him anymore. I waited long enough. He never makes anything clear." You figure, "I don't have the time or money. I need to fight to get a job, and it would be better if it's not here because I can't stand living in this prison anymore, I don't even get my space. My father isn't supporting me anymore and everything in my house is about money, money, money." You keep things to yourself because no one will help, no one will agree and no one will even understand.

This love stupid love,
has always been so rough.
All it had bought was pain,
there was no sun to stop the rain.

Why did I fall in love?,
now I need to act tough.
Sometimes I would break and cry.
Is it because I'm sick of lies?
He's not worth all the tears I cried!

Why do I do this to myself?,
that just hurts myself.
His friends and drinks are more important at this stage,
I don't know how to control this rage.

He has been very insensitive and immature,
that's why he can stand straight on the floor.

Any man is not worth my heart and soul,
because at the very end he won't rely on hope,
and will let go of the rope.
You'll fall flat to the floor,
and he'll walk out of your door.

The test

You call a hotel in Durban. A woman answers the phone and you say, "Good morning, my name is Saesha. I am looking for a job, and just recently qualified in Hotel operations and management." "She tells you, "We don't have any vacancies," and hangs up. You are now tired of the amount of people turning you down for a job. "They are all the same," you tell yourself. "No one wants to give me an opportunity. They shut the door in my face before I can even start to prove myself." The next day you change your tactics. You have so many numbers on your paper and can't see clearly which ones you called and which ones are left. You call a hotel and you are not sure if you already called the number, but think, "What's the worst they can tell me. No again, or you called us yesterday." You think, "Well if the same person answers, than surely I'll recognize the voice and hang up." A man picks up and you say, "Good morning, my name is Saesha. I am looking for a job, and just recently qualified in Hotel operations and management. If you don't have a vacancy for me, I am also prepared to do practicals with a small salary and to get some more experience at the same time." He says, "It would be nice to have a trainee here, and it sounds interesting. We haven't done anything like this before." He offers you six hundred rands to work there and says, "If it works out, you can work here for longer." After finding Vivek's briefcase, you really want to go to the United Kingdom. You are excited and calculate how long it will take you to make 20 thousand Rands to go to United Kingdom. When you look at how long it can take you, you think, "Wow that's long, and that's not even including the ticket. Two

272

years, anything can happen in two years." You are a little dissappointed but this is all you have so you take what you get, at least you'll be out of here. You say, "When I make that money from the Hotel I will move straight away to United Kingdom. I won't see them again."

So here you are, telling your family that you will move to Durban. You don't think you will ever see them again. Abhay doesn't like the idea and says, "You going to become like one of them, a Duban night." People here in Johannesburg make fun out of the Indians who come from Durban. They laugh at the way they talk, and their accent. You tell Abhay "You think I care, at least I'll have a job."

It's the 31st of December 1997 and soon you will be going to Durban. You can't wait to start your new life.

"It's January 1998,
I am in a great state.
My plans are going great,
and I'll be home late.

Feeling good and new,
pure like dew.

I can drive a car,
and feel like a star.

This year,
no more fear,
be adventurous, get into gear.

Be your best,
And let's beat the rest!"

You have three hundred rands left from working at Delta Spar the last time; you buy a one-way bus ticket to Durban. The plan to be in Durban starts one week from now. You know that Manav will find out, this is the final test. It's now or never for him, now you will know where you stand in his life. You think, "If he has got to react than it has to be now." You are prepared for him, you always were. You say to yourself, "If he comes and declares his undying love for me than I will stay. If he doesn't than I'll move on, it would be a clear sign that he doesn't love me."

It's the night before you're leaving, you can't wait and you have one hundred rands left in your account. There's still no sign of Manav. You need just a little more to accept that you mean nothing to him. Abhay tells you, "Wake me up when you go so that I can give you some money." You say, "No, I don't need money." He says, "Just wake me up." You leave early that morning and don't wake Abhay up. Your father drops you off at the pick up point for the bus going to Durban. You don't want to underestimate Manav, and still have hope, even in the last few minutes before leaving. Manav never comes. Your father doesn't wait around, and leaves once your luggage is inside. As the bus leaves, you say your goodbyes to the town and the people in it, "Bye, bye, for once and for all, I hope to never see you again." You get off at Durban and take another bus, a little bus, which takes you to Margate where the hotel is. The trip to Margate is beautiful. You have never seen the sea in such a long time. You tell yourself as you look at the sea, "I think I'm going to love living here!" When you arrive at the hotel, you go straight to reception and ask for the manager who offered you the job. You find him straight away.

You talk for a bit with him, he gives you the keys to your room and says, "Just enjoy the rest of the day, we'll talk tomorrow morning." Your boss seems easy going. You get the impression that the place is family owned. You see at least two houses among the chalets, a nice big pool, a lot of plants and trees, and you hear the sea, the air is so fresh. You walk around and go to the beach. It's been many years since you've seen the beach. You don't call home to tell them you arrived at the hotel in Durban and think, "They'd call me one of these days." You have your own room, it's cool, and even though your boss doesn't give you a time to come to work, you make sure that you are there early. Your boss says, "Go and have breakfast at the buffet, come back and then we'll start." You have breakfast and come back. He says, "Ok, you can go and help the housekeeping department". Right now, they are at one of the chalets. You find the room that they are busy with easily and look for the manager of that department. You know who she is straight away. She's the only white woman there among all the african women. She is in a wheel chair. She looks very strict, very bitter, has short hair and glasses. You introduce yourself to her and she starts shouting at you, "Why did you call again when I told you there are no jobs here, the African people in this department are working here for years and suddenly someone like you walks in, this will make them wonder if they are doing their jobs right!" She went on saying, "You are so skinny, look at you, it

275

seems like you won't even be capable of doing this work!" The workers are staring at you. She turns around, says something to the workers, and they all start to work. They ignore you completely. You think it's over and that they're going to show you what to do, but nothing, you just stand there. You have no place here, she doesn't let you step further into the room. The woman looks at you as if she wants you out of her sight. She doesn't want to give you work, in fact she doesn't want you here, in this place. You don't know what's going on, yet it feels like a racist attack on you. The tears just want to leave so you quickly walk to the beach, to an isolated area. You find the first few steps heading towards the isolated part of the beach sit down and cry.

"Crying in Durban

I cry at the beachside,
The place I liked yesterday became a funeral site.

Don't you have any mercy..,
To make someone you haven't given a chance,
unworthy.

I cry for an hour,
which seems forever.

I might be alone, penniless, but still lost in your words.
I don't understand, are you human, or an iceberg?

I am a mess and just passed the test...
The test of faith that never once existed to me,
even if it did I never recognised it....

I've come a long way to know that you can't fool me."

When you get your strength, you go to the manager and tell him, "I went there but the lady won't give me work." He says, "Take the day off and we'll talk tomorrow." Next morning you go to your manager again after breakfast and he says, "I don't think this is going to work out, you can stay here for the rest of the week and then go back home." You are very dissappointed.

It's strange that your family never called, and think there might be an explanation or perhaps they never did call. You are very angry about not being able to work there, and know it has something to do with yesterday, and the woman in the wheelchair. You don't feel like calling your family. You say, "I will call but for now I will leave them worried, to teach them their mistakes, they are to blame for pushing me so much." You sit on the bench of the hotel in the evening and look at the sea. The view of the sea is clear; the hotel is on a hill with the beach below. You look at the navy ships while you sit on the bench and wonder to yourself, "Perhaps when I get home I should consider joining the South African Navy." You wonder, "What if everything here worked out the way I thought it would work out? My family could come and visit me, and my parents would love this place, and they would love sitting here just looking at the sea." You try and look for a job during the week in the neighbouring hotels, but you have no luck. You enjoy your time at the beach; you don't know when you'll get to see it again.

"The waves seem to have a silver lining,
with the early morning sun shining.

They rise up, so high and mighty,
and this morning they land so smooth and softly.

The blue, the view, waves renew,
Once you return, what's shall become of you?"

It is almost the end of the week; you don't want to go
home. Your family didn't even call to see if you arrived
safe, or if you were ok. You need to buy your ticket to
go home. You don't have enough money to buy a ticket
back home because you know you only have one
hundred rands. You go to the bank and find three
hundred rands in your account. You know Abhay put
the money into your account. You love your brother
just as much as you hate him. You didn't know he had
your bank details or if you gave it to him. You call
home and say, "Can someone come and pick me up
tomorrow", and give them the time.

"Tomorrow I'll be leaving for home,
I don't even know what tomorrow may hold.
I feel like my tomorrow is cold.

Tomorrow I get to see my friend.
I feel like I need an extra hand,
because my family won't stop going on to the end,
but I don't regret seeing Manav again!"

When you arrive home Vivek says, "We were worried
sick, Shalini called the hotel and the workers there said,
"No one with the name Saesha works and lives here."

278

Shalini said that Abhay was going to come all the way to Durban to look for you, because he thought you went missing. You know your father was worried, even though he said nothing. When he saw you, it seems like he breathed out a long breathe of relief. Ever since the Durban incident, you never got pressure again about looking for a job, even though you still try to look for a job. Knowing your father won't give you money anymore, you ask Abhay if he could pay for a correspondence course and other small courses that you're interested in taking up; Marketing and some Computer Courses. You tell Abhay, "I'll pay you back when I can." You are happy inside to see Manav, but you know what you have to do, you tell yourself, "Saesha, forget him, he did nothing, he knew you went to Durban and did nothing."

Lamiah and you get closer. Lamiah wants to lose weight, and asks you, "Would you like to come walking with me every morning?" You think, "Perhaps she'll be motivated if I come along." You say, "Yes, why not." You don't want to look at Manav anymore but it's hard not to. You see Manav three or four times in five days on your morning walks with Lamiah. Lamiah tells you, "Manav doesn't love you, you should get over him, it's been like this for many years." You say, "She's right, there's been enough proof to tell me that we never will end up together." It hurts more being in love with him and you imagine the day you'd be free from him. You stop yourself from looking through your window when he passes the house, you stop the coincidences of bumping into him, you stop coming out of your house for a while, you stop looking outside when Manav and his other friends come to see Vivek at home, and finally you stop going to Ginas' Cafe.

You wonder about the woman in the wheelchair at the hotel in Durban, and about what she told you. You wonder, "Why did she react that way?" It made you angry and still makes you angry, just thinking about various reasons why. You say to yourself, "One day I would like to go back there when I'm older to show her that I've made a better life for myself, and that she was wrong to judge me".

Spice up your life

Now you are 19 years old, you and Lamiah hang out together almost everyday. You both walk every morning for at least an hour, and then you study for a bit for your correspondence course. One beautiful day, you walk towards Lamiah's house to see her. The wind blows, you are fimiliar with this wind. Strong winds with strong feelings, it seems to bring magic with it. It's on days like these that some feelings just stay strong, it's on days like these that you often see Manav. The wind blows, things are really strong today. As you walk towards Lamiah's house, you see Manav from afar and he sees you. You don't walk too fast, neither too slow. You don't let him change your pace. You are pretty sure that he'll slow down if he thought he'd reach his friends house quicker than you. That's what you both normally do, just so that you could see each other from afar and closer for longer. You predict that he'll reach the entrance of his friend's house just when you get to the entrance of Lamiah's house, and it happens exactly like that. This time you have the intention to lock your eyes on to his to show him just how angry you are with him. The wind is strong, you love it when it blows this way, it runs through your skin, through your hair and almost right through your body, a kiss from the wind. He looks at you, you slow down a little and so does he, to make this moment longer. The wind blows, it's stronger now, it runs through your hair, it touches your lips, and pushes your feelings right out of you. You stand confident; the wind carves the shape of your body through your baggy T-shirt. You stare at him in his eyes for the first time, from across the road and he looks in yours, with no fear you make a look that is sharp, intense, quick, angry and unlocked his eyes from yours. Your body language and eyes says enough.

"No matter how much I'll try to ignore him,
I still love him.
All the elements of the earth will try to make it stronger
again.
When I stood outside,
and didn't expect him to come,
he came,
looking at me from afar,
just how did I know it?
The air was still,
and all of the sudden,
all the colours of the wind hit me,
it flowed right through me.
The wind never stopped for it knew that true love was
around."

A few days down the line, Vivek comes home and tells you jokingly, "Manav wants to go out with you hi hi hi." You know Vivek's character well and he knows how to make you uncomfortable and embarrassed. He knows how you'd answer when he goes on this way. You give him his answer in the same manner he gave his question. You say, "Haha, No." You never can make out if Vivek is serious or not when it comes to Manav and you. It makes you angry that Manav never comes to you himself. He doesn't tell you directly what he feels instead he goes to Vivek to get his answers. You wonder, "How does he even know if Vivek is even manipulating things. Just how would you know what messages Manav already sent and is sending with him." You lose your opportunity, you can tell from seeing

Manav. You now wonder to what extent Vivek went to keep you both apart. You realise he is separating you both and doesn't ever want you both to be together. You can't believe that your brother is capable of doing something like this to his own sister. You lose your first opportunity and look at it as the last opportunity to be with Manav. You wonder, "My brother lives with me, he's supposed to be my brother, he lives in the same house as me, and yet I'm his worst enemy."

"Yesterday the day you chose,
made so much difference than you know.
I played as if I didn't care,
and you decided to do something rare.
It bought back how much I feel,
you gave me your looks that were so real.
Then you had all the guts,
bet your friends would go nuts.
Today I sit and think,
what joy it would bring.
Now all has been shattered,
and again I'm left torn and tattered.
Wish you had done what you thought,
because now I'm hurt a lot.
I thought I will get over you,
but again I'm falling back in love with you.
In fact love was always there,
but it's much stronger than you even care.
Now what am I supposed to do,
everything depends on you."

You write poetry and train yourself to write on a topic so that you become constant and don't let your thoughts go without putting it on paper. You continue for some

283

months and than it automatically starts to flow out of you. You start to keep a pen and paper under your pillow. Most thoughts come at night just when you go to sleep, than without any light you take out the paper and imagine you are writing straight, than after ten minutes another thought. You say, "I mean if I continue this way I will never end up sleeping," You now learn to control the thoughts because they just won't stop. In the mornings you look at the paper, some writing overlaps others and almost all the time they are slanted. You put them into date order and start to give each one a number.

You want to be the best poet that ever exists, and hope to be just as good as Shakespeare one day. Reading Shakespeare's work always gives you inspiration. Often you write the best things about love drawing out suppressed feelings of the love you have for Manav. It doesn't take long and it isn't difficult for something good to come out when writing about love. Shalini gives you some money to buy some things like shoes or pants. You don't do much shopping at this time but still have things that look good. Lamiah talks about "Allah" a lot. You don't know anyone who talks so much about "Allah." Her faith is so big, so strong, that it helps you find a great universal power, which most people call God. You accept your life, no matter how many dreams you have, you accept this situation, and don't fight it anymore. You stop trying hard at looking for a job. You tell yourself, "Why make yourself suffer if you've done your best." You trust this higher being, you trust that he or she has your best interest at heart.

You get into pop music and now and again, you and

Shalini dance around in the salon. You know all the artists and all the songs and sing along. Your mum also enjoys the music you're listening to, she seems happy and hates your dad's golden oldies, she even tells Shalini to tell your dad not to put it on since it makes her depressed. Unconciously you train your voice and automatically learn to be in tunc. You are comfortable to sing around your mum and your sister. Shalini also starts to sing.

You: *"Colours of the world,"*
Shalini: *"Spice up your life."*
You: *"Every boy and every girl,"*
Shalini: *"Spice up your life."*
You: *"People of the world."*
Shalini: *"Spice up you life."*
You and Shalini: *Ahhhhhhhhhhh................ la la la, lalala la la la, la la la lalalalaaaaaaaaaa*

When Abhay hears you two singing he makes fun out of you both, even if you are both good. He screams from the other end of the house, "Shut up, if you don't know how to sing!" The spice girls are great hits during this time and your favourite one from the group is Mel B, Sporty Spice.

Shalini buys you the platforms the fake ones, which are going for cheap, because the real ones for name and brand is just too expensive. At times, you comb your hair like Mel B. Abhay asks one day, "So what's this style?" You say the "Spice Girls style, Sporty Spice." When Lamiah and you hang around, she is always observing men. One day, you go to her friend's shop. Some teenage boys walk in, and when they leave,

Lamiah says something about one of the guys. You answer and say, "I didn't notice". Lamiah says, "You never look at men and seem so uninterested."

Your dad gives you and Shalini some money for your driving lessons. You take lessons with Jayesh's friend. It's the second time you sit in the car with Shalini driving. Shalini has changed so much, she was so brave once upon a time, people just put her down so much. She just submerged into letting them get away with it. She doesn't fight for her rights and allows people to tell her what they want and most of all they seem to get away with it. Your father gets angry when you both ask him for money for the exam. He gives you both the money, but then says, "This is the last time and then no more." You both make it to the driving exam together. You and Shalini pray hard, you both wish to get your licence. You wonder about how you tried getting your driving licence with a good teacher and regret not having four hundred rands on your first test, to pay off the man who tested you, ever since both you and Shalini put a fortune into driving lessons and exams. Now here you are, both you and Shalini. You both try for the last time and you both fail the exam. You both don't want to give up and your father doesn't want to give you both money anymore. Shalini pays with her own money for more lessons for both you and her. She even pays for another exam. Finally, you both pass that exam and get your licences. You consider redoing your passport, since your father put his name as your second name in your passport and Vivek's passport. You think he made a mistake. You have the choice to change the names now, and you wish to leave it as Shaesha and your last name. You really don't like that his name is your middle name. You don't have enough money to make the change, and you decide to leave your father's name in your passport because most certificates you have has your father's name in them.

It's October 2002. Apparently, the life jacket can injure your mouth and nose really badly. You place one hand across the jacket and hold it down, you use the other hand to close your nostrils. You have to jump into the water, you have no choice. You look at a girl who doesn't know how to swim, she is so nervous to jump and think to yourself, "Lucky I did the swimming course, otherwise I don't think I'll have the guts to do this." You try to position yourself, since it's your first time jumping from such an altitude. You take a deep breath and jump. You now have to swim to the boat, you manage it with your bad swimming skills but can't seem to get onto the boat. You try to pull yourself up once, but slide off and now try even harder but still can't get in. It's the third time trying now, you try to lift yourself up. "Wow this time it seems so easy," you think until finding yourself in the boat. Someone grabbed you by your life jacket and dragged you in.

Lightning Source UK Ltd.
Milton Keynes UK
UKOW02f0818150914

238568UK00001B/3/P